First Steps
WITH
RISC OS 6

by David Bradforth, Aaron Timbrell and David Holden

First Steps with RISC OS 6

Published by
David Bradforth
16 Rodney Way
Romford
Essex
RM7 8PD

Email: david.bradforth@alligatagroup.com

Printed by CreateSpace, an Amazon.com company.

Published by Alligata Media, Romford.

ISBN-13: 978-1502811332
ISBN-10: 1502811332

About the Authors

David Bradforth is an established technical author, having been responsible for the creation and publication of titles such as *eBay Advisor, Website Designer* and *Essential OpenOffice.org*. He has been involved with the RISC OS market for over twenty years, having first been published in *Acorn Computing* magazine at the age of 15.

Aaron Timbrell is the founder and Director of 3QD Developments Ltd; which took the rights to RISC OS over from RISCOS Ltd within the last couple of years. The company also supplies the VirtualAcorn range of emulators allowing PC and Mac OS X users to run RISC OS within the desktop.

Dave Holden was the founder of APDL, the Archimedes Public Domain Library. APDL was a significant supplier of software and hardware for the RISC OS platform. The company began a major expansion in the early 1990s, taking over The DataStream, Arch Angel and The Datafile PD libraries and supplying a significant hardware catalogue. In the early 2000's, working in partnership with David Bradforth, APDL began acquiring software rights from Beebug, Clares Micro Supplies, Pineapple Software, The Fourth Dimension and others. David Holden died in May 2014; a tribute to his work is online at www.apdl.org.uk.

About the Authors

David Bradforth is an established technical author, having been responsible for the creation and publication of titles such as *eBay Advisor, Website Designer* and *Essential OpenOffice.org*. He has been involved with the RISC OS market for over twenty years, having first been published in *Acorn Computing* magazine at the age of 15.

Aaron Timbrell is the founder and Director of 3QD Developments Ltd; which took the rights to RISC OS over from RISCOS Ltd within the last couple of years. The company also supplies the VirtualAcorn range of emulators allowing PC and Mac OS X users to run RISC OS within the desktop.

Dave Holden was the founder of APDL, the Archimedes Public Domain Library. APDL was a significant supplier of software and hardware for the RISC OS platform. The company began a major expansion in the early 1990s, taking over The DataStream, Arch Angel and The Datafile PD libraries and supplying a significant hardware catalogue. In the early 2000's, working in partnership with David Bradforth, APDL began acquiring software rights from Beebug, Clares Micro Supplies, Pineapple Software, The Fourth Dimension and others. David Holden died in May 2014; a tribute to his work is online at www.apdl.org.uk.

Dedication

This book is dedicated to those who are running RISC OS 6 on their Acorn A7000+, Risc PC or Virtual Acorn. And to those who are yet to run it, visit www.riscos.com.

Authors' Acknowledgements

We are deeply grateful to Aaron Timbrell and David Holden for their assistance in the preparation of this book. It started as First Steps with RISC OS 4, published approximately ten years ago; then was updated and published as part of the RISC OS 6 online user guide. It has never appeared in printed form until now, so we hope you like the end result.

We are grateful to 3QD Developments Ltd / RISCOS.com for their agreement to the updated book being released.

Contents

Introduction

RISC OS has evolved over the years to gain a reputation as one of the most user friendly operating systems available. However for those new to an operating system even the most simple things appearing on the screen could be confusing. This is where the First Steps with RISC OS 6 guide comes in. It shows you how to use RISC OS 6 and the desktop.

This book will not cover the built in applications suite as these applications are covered in their own section of the online documentation. Neither will it show you how to configure RISC OS, as this is also covered in a separate section. What this guide will explain is the principles on which RISC OS is based and also how to use RISC OS. Even if you have used RISC OS before there will be new features that you haven't seen before so we recommend that even experienced users read the documentation.

Assumptions

With this guide we are making the assumption that RISC OS Six is installed and working on your computer. You might have a computer with RISC OS Six pre-installed or you might have upgraded to RISC OS Six through the RISCOS Ltd Select Scheme. So this guide will not show you how to install RISC OS Six, you should follow the installation instructions provided. If you are not running RISC OS Six already then you will need to install it before reading this guide as some sections will not apply to earlier versions of RISC OS.

Getting help

The !Help application provides on-screen information as you use your computer. You can use this to get help on the desktop and most applications. For more information refer to the Help section in the appendix of this guide.

1. Getting started

Switching on

When you switch on your RISC OS computer it will perform a small number of system self tests, during which you may notice the screen change from one colour to another. Normally these will all run through quickly and without incident, in which case the RISC OS Boot sequence will begin.

RISC OS Six currently softloads over the top of RISC OS 4.XX, so you will briefly see a softloading message, followed by a clearing of the screen and then you will be presented with a screen resembling that below.

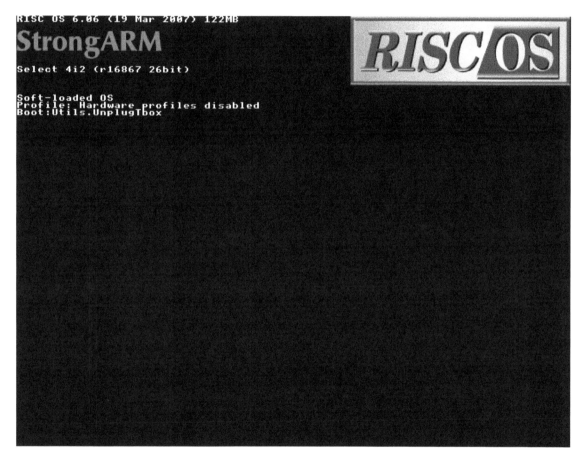

This part of the Boot sequence is sometimes referred to as the PreDesk section, as this sets up various parts of your RISC OS environment prior to entering the RISC OS graphical Desktop.

If RISC OS fails to boot correctly, you may be presented with the Boot Menu (see the Appendix section of the guide for more details). This may be due to incorrect configuration of the system and which device is the selected boot device.

Once RISC OS Six has loaded you will be presented with the RISC OS desktop. This will look something like the picture here:

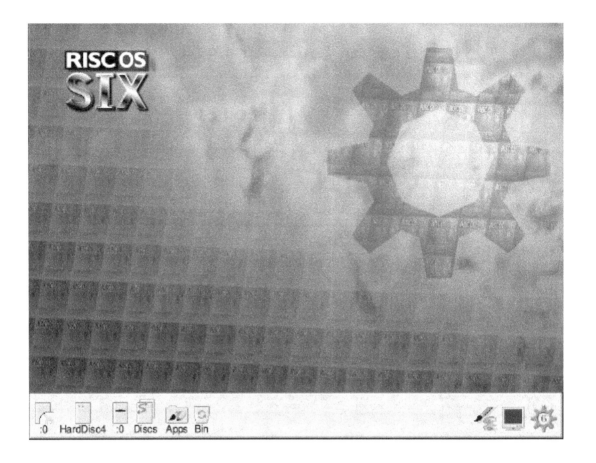

The bar running across the bottom of the screen is referred to as the 'Icon Bar'. It is from this area that you can gain access to CDs, floppy discs, your hard disc drive and any applications that you may have already loaded onto the desktop.

At the left side of the iconbar is a series of icons relating to file and disc access - i.e. the way in which you can access your data and applications through the RISC OS desktop. The appearance of these icons may vary slightly from those shown. These icons are:

CD ROM drive. This icon will only be present if your computer is fitted with a CD ROM drive. Using this you can either open the content of data or application CD-ROMs, such as those supplied by software publishers, or, if there is an audio CD in the drive, then simply clicking on this icon will start it playing.

Hard Disc drive. The hard disc contains all of your data, any applications that you have installed onto the computer and any temporary files required by RISC OS applications for safe operation. We explain later on how you can make use of your hard disc, either to launch applications or to store data.

Note that some machines may be fitted with more than one hard drive so there may be more than just one hard drive icon. Also the name under the icon shows the name given to the drive, so yours may not be 'HardDisc4' it might be 'IDEDisc4' or have some other name.

Floppy Disc drive. If your machine is fitted with a floppy disc drive then you can click on this icon to open a floppy disc that has been inserted into the floppy disc drive.

Network icon. This will be present if your computer is equipped with networking facilities, either on-board or via a third party plug in interface. It is used to access disc drives on other computers connected to your network.

Apps icon. The Apps icon opens a special folder stored within RISC OS itself. This contains applications which are supplied as part of RISC OS such as Draw and Paint and also links to certain other applications such as those stored in the Apps folder on your main hard disc. See Chapter 12 for more information on this.

The right hand side of the iconbar contains further icons. Clicking on these icons will normally open a program window relating to the icon you've clicked on.

There may be a number of icons here, but for now we will cover the Display Manager and the Task Manager.

Display Manager. Using the Display Manager you can set your computer to use a different screen display mode. A number of display modes are available, offering up to 16.7 million colours.

Task Manager. The Task Manager provides a breakdown of the memory usage by different parts of the operating system.

The Mouse

This small but vital part of the system usually consists of a box with three or more buttons on the top and either a nylon ball underneath or an optical reader. For the mouse to work it should be kept in contact with a flat surface and it is recommended that you acquire a suitable mouse mat as they have the correct surface for optimum performance from your mouse.

The mouse buttons are given names under RISC OS.

- Left - **SELECT**
- Middle - **MENU**
- Right - **ADJUST**

Throughout this manual the mouse buttons will be referred to by these names and shown in heavy type so something like 'press **MENU**' or 'click **MENU**' would mean press the middle mouse button.

Hold the mouse with the lead pointing away from you. Move the mouse and you will see an arrow shaped pointer moving around the screen. When you move the mouse to the right the pointer moves to the right and when you move it to the left it moves to the left. When you move the mouse away from you the pointer moves up the screen and when you move it towards you it moves down.

The Keyboard

The keyboard is divided into three parts.

First the **Qwerty** section, so named because the first six letters on the top row of alphabetical keys in this section of the keyboard are QWERTY. This is almost identical to a typewriter keyboard, although there are a few additional, computer specific, keys.

Secondly the **Numeric keypad.** This is the series of calculator style keys at the right hand side of the keyboard and is primarily used for typing numbers.

Thirdly there are the **Special Keys.** These are the collection of keys between the Qwerty and Numeric sections where amongst others, you will find the **Arrow keys**. There is also a single row of keys along the top of the keyboard which are called the **Function Keys.**

Numeric Keypad

You will notice that when you switch the machine on a **Num Lock** light appears at the top of the numeric keypad. This should normally be left on. If the light goes out, simply press the **Num Lock key** to switch it on. You will see that this numeric keypad has the addition (+), minus (-), division (/) and multiplication (*) symbols and well as the decimal point or full stop - (the same key). There is also an **Enter** key which behaves in exactly the same way as the **Return** key on the main keyboard. This applies to all the keys on the numeric keypad in that their function or effect is the same as the equivalent key on the main keyboard.

Note, however, that although the function of the keys on the numeric keypad is normally the same as the keys on the main part of the keyboard with some specific programs the action of the numeric keys may be slightly different.

Main Keyboard

This contains the keys normally found on a qwerty keyboard plus some additional ones.

There are two **Shift** keys, used to produce Capital or Upper Case letters or the upper symbol on a key where there are two different symbols. for example, % on the number **5** key on the main keyboard.

There are two **Control** keys - marked **Ctrl** . Like **Shift** these are not used on their own but in combination with another key. Programs often use **Ctrl** with another key to perform specific functions. Making a program perform an action using a keypress is known as a **keyboard shortcut.**

There are also two **Alt** keys. These are not normally employed by programs, but when used in conjunction with the numeric keypad can insert the ASCII code for a key into the keyboard buffer, thereby allowing you to 'type' characters which do not appear on the keyboard. For example, to obtain the copyright symbol © hold down either **Alt** key and type the number 169 into the *numeric* keypad then release the **Alt** key. Do the same with the number 174 for the trademark symbol ®.

Special keys

These are in two groups; in a line along the top of the keyboard and a group of keys between the QWERTY keyboard and the numeric keypad.

At the top of the keyboard are a series of twelve **Function Keys** labelled **F1** to **F12** . These perform various functions with different pieces of software, often in conjunction with the **Shift** or **Ctrl** keys.

Many of these functions are common to most well written programs. For example, **F3** will normally initiate a Save function, **F4** is often some sort of Search, and **F8** will Undo the last action.

Function key **F12** will, under normal circumstances, exit the desktop temporarily and produce a blank line at the bottom of the screen to give you access to the *Command Line Interpreter* (CLI). Here you can type commands which are passed directly to the Operating System. Because the prompt used is an asterisk, as it was with the old BBC computer, these are often referred to as **Star Commands.**

You can exit this function and return to normal desktop operation by just pressing the **Return** key twice.

You should note that when you press **F12** the mouse pointer will disappear. This is because you are no longer in the desktop. Although you can probably still see most of the desktop it's completely inactive until you have pressed **Return** twice to exit command line mode.

An alternative is **Ctrl-F12.** This means hold down the **Ctrl** key and press **F12**. This will open a *Task Window,* which provides a similar function but within a desktop window, so you don't need to exit the desktop.

Try pressing either **F12** or **Ctrl-F12** and typing **CAT** or **cat** followed by the **Return** key. This will provide a list (or CATalogue) of the disc contents. When you are ready to return to the desktop, press **Return** if you just pressed **F12** or, if you used a Task Window close it by clicking on its close icon.

Between the numeric keypad and the main QWERTY keyboard are a group of keys which you will use frequently. The **Arrow keys** are also known as **Cursor keys.** The cursor is the point at which you can enter characters on the screen. Its shape can vary but it is usually shaped like a capital 'I' in red, and in this form is referred to as the **caret** .

There are six keys directly above the cursor keys. These are used by applications, and the function they perform will depend upon the specific program.

2. The WIMP

. . . .

Windows, Icons, Menus and Pointer

We will now explore the **WIMP** environment.

Move the mouse pointer over the top of the HardDisc4 disc drive icon and click the **SELECT** button.

To clarify this, the **Active Point** of the mouse pointer is the tip of the arrow, so place this point approximately in the centre of the icon you wish to select When you press a mouse button don't hold it down (unless you are *dragging* an object - see later), just click it and release it quickly. The wimp may interpret a long press of the mouse button differently to a sharp click.

When you click on the hard drive icon the hard disc light should come on momentarily, indicating that the disc is operating. A window will then open on the screen showing you what is on the disc, in *icon* or picture format. The window you have just opened should look something like this.

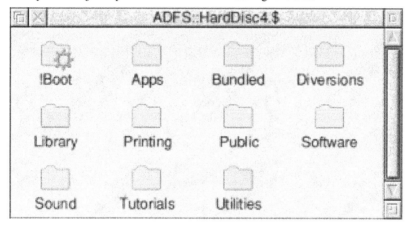

This window (or **directory viewer** as it is properly called) has several characteristics that are common to almost all the windows you will encounter using RISC OS, no matter what version.

The **Title Bar** is always at the top of the window, and contains the title of the file or the directory you are looking at. The window shown has the title **ADFS::HardDisc4.$**

You can now explore some of the features of RISC OS windows. In all cases click the **SELECT** button unless directed otherwise.

A skill you will need to learn is **Double-Clicking.** A double click means clicking a mouse button twice in rapid succession while pointing at an icon. It is important that you do not move the mouse between clicks.

You can close the window by clicking on the **Close Icon**. This is the small cross towards the left hand end of the Title bar. If you close a window it will vanish from the screen.

You can move a window around the screen and position it where you wish. Do this by pointing the mouse anywhere on the title bar and clicking and holding down the **SELECT** button while at the same time moving the mouse around the screen. This procedure is known as **dragging** and is an important technique you will need to develop to use the desktop and RISC OS programs. The window should move instantly when you drag the mouse. This facility for re-positioning is important because you will often find yourself with several windows on the screen and you will need to be able to move them around. Drag the window up towards the top of the screen and release the button.

The **Toggle Size** icon is found at the top right hand corner of the window. Clicking **SELECT** on this icon will expand the window to the full width of the screen, or as wide as is required to show everything within the window (see below). If everything in the window is already visible the toggle size icon will have no effect.

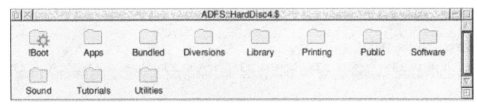

The **Adjust Size** icon is at the bottom right hand corner of the window. Clicking and dragging this icon (that is, put the mouse pointer over the icon, press and hold down the **SELECT** button while moving the mouse) will allow you to move the bottom corner of the window, thus altering its shape. This is useful if you wish to make the window small and thin to perhaps tuck it out of the way at the edge of the screen. Try dragging the **Adjust size** icon towards the left of the screen and then downwards to create a tall, thin window. Notice that the contents re-organise and remain in alphabetical order. Now click on the **Toggle Size** icon a couple of times to see the effect.

Return the window to a tall thin shape. Use the **Adjust Size** icon if necessary. Now move the **Adjust Size** icon up towards the top of the window until the window only shows the top three icons. You will now be able to see what is known as the **Scroll Bar** down the right hand side of the window. This looks like an elevator in a lift shaft. Click the **SELECT** button on the arrow at the foot of the scroll bar and see how the scroll bar moves down and the 'view' into the window moves with it. If you click on the arrow at the top of the scroll bar the view will move up. Now if you do the same thing using the **ADJUST** button you will see that the bar moves in the opposite directions. Alternatively you can drag the scroll bar itself up and down the shaft.

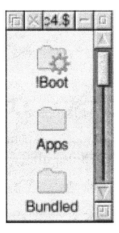

The picture below shows a desktop window with its main features illustrated. The **iconise icon** may not be present in your windows but this function can still be used as described below.

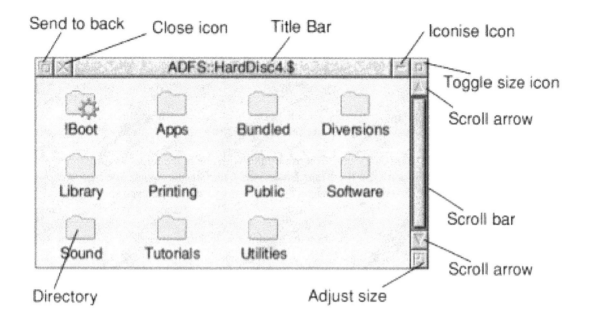

Send to back   Close icon   Title Bar   Iconise Icon

ADFS::HardDisc4.$

Toggle size icon

Scroll arrow

!Boot   Apps   Bundled   Diversions

Library   Printing   Public   Software

Scroll bar

Sound   Tutorials   Utilities

Scroll arrow

Directory   Adjust size

You can convert any current window to an icon on the desktop. This is useful for temporary space saving, but does not save your data unless you save it yourself, so if you are using a program to complete some work we recommend you save your data before experimenting. Click on the **iconise** icon or, if there is no iconise icon, then click on the **close** icon whilst holding down the **Shift** key. The current window will close and appear as an icon on the desktop backdrop. Exactly where the iconised icon will appear depends upon how your computer is configured (*see later chapter*).To reopen the window to its full size double-click on the icon.

The icon **Apps** on the screen is also a directory. To open this directory and see its contents move the pointer over the top of the Apps icon on the icon bar and click the **SELECT** button. This should open another window. If you also have the original directory viewer open your screen should now look similar to this with the windows overlapping.

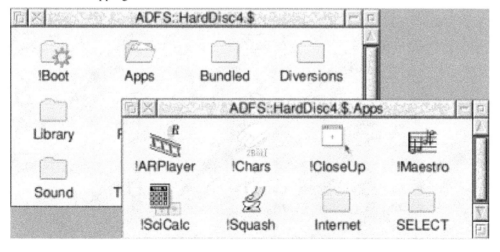

ADFS::HardDisc4.$

!Boot   Apps   Bundled   Diversions

Library   F

Sound   T

ADFS::HardDisc4.$.Apps

!ARPlayer   !Chars   !CloseUp   !Maestro

!SciCalc   !Squash   Internet   SELECT

You can now use another window feature to alter the order in which the windows appear, the **Send to Back** icon at the top left hand corner. Click **SELECT** on the send to back icon and the window will go to the back, that is, behind the other window.

You can easily bring a window to the front by clicking **SELECT** on its title bar, assuming that you can see it.

Directories and Folders

The word *Directory* actually refers to the way that files are arranged on your hard drive and the word *Folder* describes the way that this is represented visually in the Wimp by the icons which resemble the folders used in office filing.

These two words are now used interchangeably, so both in this book and elsewhere phrases like 'open the directory' and 'open the folder' can be taken to mean the same thing.

To 'open' a folder just double-click on its icon. You can try this with one of the folder icons in the HardDisc4 viewer window (but don't use !Boot) the **Diversions** folder would probably be a good choice. When you double-click on the Diversions folder icon a new directory viewer will open showing its contents.

You can use the 'click and drag' process to position the windows so that they are side by side or one above the other.

So far you have used the **SELECT** button to carry out all the above tasks. If you use **ADJUST** you will see slightly different results.

Close the Diversions directory viewer again by clicking on its close icon. Now double-click on the Diversions folder icon again but this time use the **ADJUST** button instead of **SELECT** . A new window showing the contents of the Diversions directory will open just as before, but this time the previous window, the HardDisc4 directory viewer, will have closed leaving you with only the Diversions directory viewer open.

If you now use the **ADJUST** button on the close icon to close the Diversions directory viewer you will see that the window closes but the previous window, or **Parent window,** reopens.

3. *Menus and Windows*

···

Using menus

If you put the mouse pointer over a directory viewer window and click the **MENU** button the filer menu will appear. This will be described in a later chapter, but it will serve as an example of the type of menu structure that is used by many RISC OS programs.

Some of the options on these menus have arrows to their right, and you will find these on many other RISC OS menus. This means that this item has a *sub-menu* . To open the sub-menu move the mouse pointer over the arrow and the sub-menu will appear. You can then slide the pointer onto the sub-menu to make a selection.

Moving menus

A menu has a title bar just like most windows, and, just as with the window, you can drag a menu by placing the mouse pointer on the menu's title bar and holding down the **SELECT** button.

Menus and ADJUST

If you click on an item on a menu with the **SELECT** button then you will have found that the menu will vanish from the screen. Menus are not intended to remain on screen, and clicking the mouse anywhere outside the menu will close it.

Although this is normally what is required there may be times, for example, if you want to select two items from the same menu, when you don't want the menu to close immediately you make your selection. If you click on a menu item with the **ADJUST** button instead of **SELECT** then you will find that the menu will remain open, thus allowing you to make further selections if required.

This should happen with all well-behaved RISC OS programs.

Ticked items on menus

Some items on a menu may have a tick to their left. This is used where a menu is a list of options, one or more of which may be switched *On* or *Off*. The tick then indicates which items on the menu are selected.

Menu shortcuts

With many programs operations can be selected either from a menu or by using a shortcut keypress. Often, to act as a reminder to the user that a shortcut exists, the key or keys that have to be pressed to perform the same operation as selecting the item from the menu are shown on the menu.

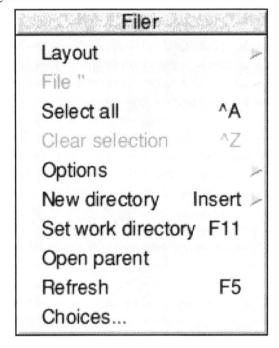

These will normally appear on the right hand side of the menu item, and there are a couple of symbols that are used when you need to press a key with the **Ctrl** or **Shift** key held, or sometimes both of these.

The ^ character is shorthand for the **Ctrl** key and an upward pointing arrow ⇑ is shorthand for the **Shift** key. Both of these together ^ ⇑ would mean press and hold down both **Ctrl** and **Shift** while you press the required key.

For example **F4** would mean that pressing the function key **F4** would have the same effect as selecting that item from the menu.

⇑ **F4** would mean hold down the **Shift** key and press **F4** .

Click to open sub-menus

It is possible to configure your RISC OS computer to open sub-menus when clicked on, rather than automatically when the mouse moves over the sub-menu arrow or (when configured) the pointer stays over the menu item for a period of time. How to configure this is described in the configuration section of the manual, but here the modified behaviour is described.

Clicking to open sub-menus is more natural for touch screens or similar devices. Mouse operation is, of course supported, but modified slightly.

To open a sub-menu when this feature is enabled, either click on the sub-menu arrow at the side of the menu or click the **MENU** button on the item itself. Once the sub-menu opens, its parent becomes locked until either a selection is made or the menu is cancelled by clicking elsewhere on the screen.

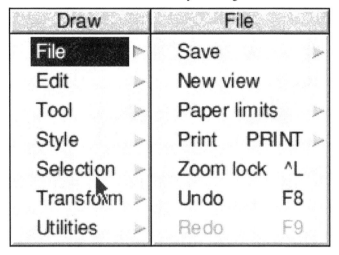

If the mouse pointer happens to pass over the parent menu, this does not affect the opened sub-menu. To change to a different sub-menu, another click is required. The open sub-menu is indicated in the parent menu by a frozen highlight and by the arrows at the side; all arrows will be raised, except for the one with an open sub-menu.

Selecting objects in windows

Before we can proceed you need to understand how objects are 'selected' under RISC OS. Although the following description describes how objects are selected and de-selected in a filer window the same principles apply with most other types of window you will encounter.

If you place the mouse pointer over any of the icons in a filer window and click **SELECT** you will see that it becomes inverted. as shown in the picture. The left hand icon here is selected, and this means that any actions you initiate will be carried out on the selected object or, if more than one is selected, objects.

To de-select an object click on it with the **ADJUST** button. Another way to de-select items is to click with **SELECT** anywhere in an empty or blank part of the window. This will de-select all items currently selected, not just one as with clicking with **ADJUST**.

Selecting multiple objects

If you click with **SELECT** on an object while one is already selected the second will become selected and the first will be de-selected. If you want to select more than one object at a time there are two ways this can be done. The first is known as *rubber banding* as it is analogous with stretching a rubber band round a group of objects.

Place the mouse pointer at the corner of an imaginary square which will contain all the objects you want to select. Hold down the **SELECT** button and drag the mouse pointer to the diagonally opposite corner of this imaginary square and release the mouse button. You will see that as you move the pointer a box, drawn in dotted lines, will appear.

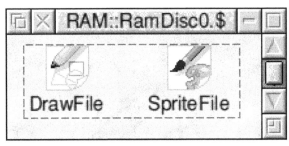

When you release the mouse button all the icons that were inside (or partially inside) this 'box' will become selected.

The second way of selecting multiple objects is to click on them with the **ADJUST** button. If you use **ADJUST** instead of **SELECT** when you select an object then it becomes selected just as normal, but any other objects already selected don't become de-selected.

You can only select multiple objects in the same filer window. As soon as you select an object in a different filer window any objects selected in the previous window will be de-selected.

It's worth spending a bit of time playing around selecting and de-selecting groups of objects. There are many variations on the ways you can do this, for example, if you want to select almost all of a block of files you can select the block by rubber banding and then de-select any you don't require by clicking on them with **ADJUST** .

Types of icons and buttons

There are various types of icons you will find in windows, but they can be divided into two main categories, *passive* and *active*.

Passive icons are those which you can't affect by clicking on them. They are normally there to impart some sort of information and don't require any interaction by the user.

Active icons are those which are used to get input from the user. Normally they will be some type of button, but they can also be writable, which means you are expected to type text into them.

Making things happen

The two most common type of 'action buttons' are illustrated in this window. It's actually what appears if you try to close a document when using OvationPro without saving your work. It's a typical RISC OS *warning* window so it's ideal for showing how they work.

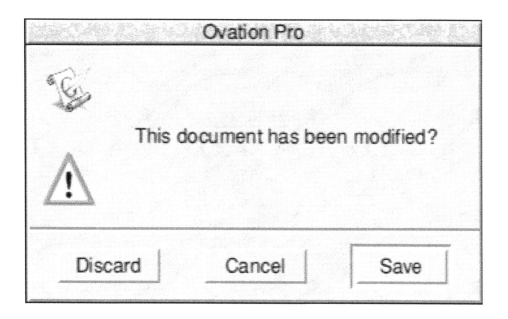

The top part of the window is a *passive* area displaying a message to tell you that you have made changes to the document and asking an implied question; *What do you want to do now?* Below this are three buttons which offer you a choice of options with which you can answer the question, and you do so by clicking on the appropriate button.

The two buttons on the left labelled **Discard** and **Cancel** are *Action Buttons*, that is, when you click on them some action will be performed. The button on the right labelled **Save** is also an Action button but it's a special type of action button known as the **Default action button**. As you can see its appearance is different from the other buttons since it looks as if it has a raised edge. With most windows of this type whatever action is specified by the default action button will carried out if you press the **Return** key as well as if you click on the button with the mouse.

Making choices

Quite often you will need to set options or choices and a window and there are two special types of button for doing this. Both of them have two states, **On** and **Off**. The buttons will toggle between the two states when clicked on. As well as letting you make a choice you can also see, from the appearance of the button, what the current state is.

These buttons are divided into two types, the **Option** button and the **Radio** button. The illustrations show the standard RISC OS icons for these buttons, but some programs, especially older ones, may use their own individual designs.

Option buttons both indicate whether an option is *On* or *Off* and let you switch between the two states by clicking on the button. They normally appear as shown, with the 'pushed in' or *On* state on the left and the 'out' or *Off* state on the right.

Radio buttons work differently from Option buttons. The name comes from the waveband selection buttons used on old portable radios where pushing in one button makes all the others pop out. Radio buttons are always used in groups and clicking on any button in the group de-selects all the others.

Some programs may use the Radio icon in place of the Option icon. This is purely cosmetic and it will behave like an Option button.

Writable icons

These are icons into which the user can type text. They are used where the program requires more than just an on/off input. They are often (but not necessarily) distinguished by having a white background whereas icons which just display information usually have a pale grey background.

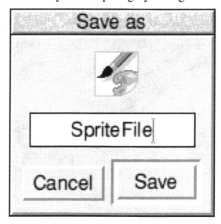

Usually the program will place the caret in the icon ready for you to type into it, if not, just click the mouse with the pointer over the icon and the caret will appear in the icon.

Often you will find that you can only type certain characters into a writable icon. For example, if you are expected to type a number then only the figures 0 to 9 might be allowed and letters will be ignored.

You can use the left and right arrows to move backwards and forwards along the line and the **Backspace** and **Delete** keys to delete characters.**Ctrl-Left Arrow** and **Ctrl-Right Arrow** will move to the start and end of the line respectively.

To delete all the text in the icon use **Ctrl-U**

Where a window has a number of writable icons into which you are expected to enter text, for example, a name and address, then you can usually move backwards and forwards between them using the Up and Down arrow keys. Also you may find that if you press **Return** after entering text in one icon the caret will automatically move to the next.

Where there is a *Default Action Button* in a window then pressing **Return** with the caret in the last writable icon in the window will often act as if you had clicked on this button.

4. The Floppy Disc Drive

RISC OS computers which have a floppy disc drive make use of 3½ inch discs. Note that the A9 computer does not have a floppy disc drive. For machines running VirtualAcorn products this section only applies to computers that have an internal IDE floppy drive, it does not apply to machines with an external USB floppy drive as these cannot read RISC OS discs.

Although floppy discs are very robust they do need some care:

- Always treat your discs with respect and handle them carefully

- Keep them in a safe place away from dusty environments.

- Do not touch the inner part of the disc which you can expose by opening the metal slider.

- Keep the discs away from magnetic forces and power cables.

The disc will only fit into the drive one way. Insert the edge with the metal slider into the drive with the arrow on the front of the disc to the left and the 'cut off' corner to the right. If you try to insert a disc wrongly it won't go into the drive fully. Don't force it or you will damage the drive.

The disc has a write protect slider which works like the tabs you can break off music or video cassettes to prevent accidental over-recording or erasure. The slider can cover or uncover a hole. If you can see through the hole then the disc is **write protected** this means that information can only be **read** from the disc and not **written** to it.

In computer terms when you write to a disc you put or record something onto it, in other words you **save** something. If the disc is write protected you will not be able to save anything onto it but you will be able to load programs and files into the computer. This is known as **reading** from the disc. The terms *read* and *write* will appear often, so it is important to understand the difference.

Usually you would not wish your discs to be write protected as you may wish to save work you have done for future use. Remember that if you can see through the write protect slider then you will not be able to save or write onto the disc.

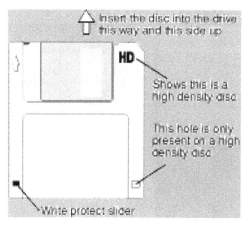

Types of disc

There are two types of disc in common usage, **Double Density** and **High Density**. A high density disc can be distinguished by the letters 'HD' either written or etched into the plastic beside the slider and it will have a square hole on the opposite side to the write protect slider.

High density discs (sometimes referred to as 'hi density') should only be used for formats greater than 1 Mb. Double density discs should only be used for formats less than 1 Mb. Most computers will not allow you to format a disc wrongly, but some models of RISC OS computers will let you override this and use an inappropriate format, so do check first. If you do use the wrong format for the type of disc it might initially appear OK but your data may not be safe and the disc may not read in another machine.

Formatting a disc

When you purchase a disc you will often find that it has been pre-formatted for use with PC computers. While RISC OS can read from and write to PC formatted discs this does have disadvantages as you can only use upper case characters with a maximum of eight letters in the filename so any applications you copy to the disc may not work.

You will therefore need to format the disc for use on RISC OS. This means that the computer will lay out the various tracks and sectors upon which data is placed and write other information to the disc which enables RISC OS to recognise it. Once a disc has been formatted for use on RISC OS it will not be readable on a PC or Mac without special software.

A PC formatted disc can be used to easily exchange files with PC owners. Using common file formats, such as TXT, GIF, JPEG etc. you can ensure that your PC owning friends can read your data, or applications such as EasiWriter will create files that natively support PC programs.

Put the disc in the drive. If you are having problems inserting the disc it's probably because there's something blocking it. Do not force it as you may damage the drive. You will have noticed that the button next to the disc drive springs out when you insert a disc. If you push in this button the disc will eject.

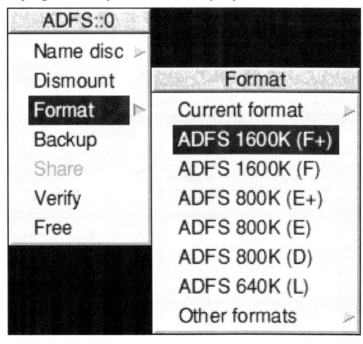

With the disc in the drive place the mouse pointer over the floppy drive icon (:0) and click the **MENU**

button. A menu will appear as shown. Move the pointer over Format then to the right over the arrow and the *Format sub-menu* will open. Move to **F+** and click **SELECT**. Using RISC OS Six you can format discs in all previous Acorn formats and also prepare discs for use on PCs and Atari ST computers. A window will open asking you to confirm that you wish to format the disc. If you do, click on **Format** and wait as the disc is formatted. If you do not, close the window and the disc will be left in its original state.

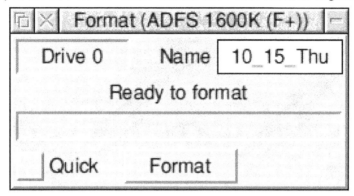

RISC OS Six includes a **Quick** formatting option. This should only be used to format discs that are known to be error free as in order to speed up the formatting some checks made by RISC OS are skipped.

Formatting takes a few minutes.

You are always asked to confirm formatting because the process is destructive of all data on the disc. Formatting completely wipes the disc with no chance of recovering anything that was on it. There is no limit to the number of times you can format a disc, but over time they can lose their data integrity.

Choice of formats

You will notice that the format menu has a number of options.

- ADFS 1600K (F+)

- ADFS 1600K (F)

- ADFS 800K (E+)

- ADFS 800K (E)

- ADFS 800K (D)

- ADFS 640K (L)

and through the Other Formats menu:

- DOS 1.44M / DOS 720K / DOS 1.2M / DOS 360K

- Atari 720K / Atari 360K

The 1600K, 800K, 720K, 640K, 360K, 1.2M and 1.44M refer to disc capacity - (K = Kilobytes, M = Megabytes). All twelve of these formats are using what is referred to as **ADFS**, or **A**dvanced **D**isc Filing **S**ystem. The **L** format was available on the BBC Master, and was the standard format used by developers releasing software for the BBC Master Compact. This format will be of interest to you if you want to exchange data with either of these machines. Most people will find no benefit at all in using the L format.

The **D** format was used by the first Archimedes computers at the time of their launch in 1987. It was later replaced by E format which should always be used in preference. It is included only to retain compatibility with early machines.

The **F** format was introduced with RISC OS 3 to support high density disc drives.

All of these formats are limited to 10 character filenames and 77 files per directory.

RISC OS Six includes a number of key extensions to these formats, especially in the support of long filenames, up to 255 characters, and almost unlimited files per directory.

E+ and **F+** formats were introduced with RISC OS 4. These remove the restrictions of 10 characters per filename and 77 files per directory. However these disc formats can only be read by machines with RISC OS 4 or later. If you want to exchange data with people with older versions of RISC OS you should not use these disc formats.

Other Formats lets you create discs that will allow data to be shared with users of other types of computer. Note that while there are a number of options available you are recommended to only use the DOS 1.44M or 720K as these can be read by almost every other computer platform.

When the disc has been formatted a window will appear telling you that formatting is complete. Click on **OK** to close the window. Put the mouse pointer over the disc drive icon (:0) and click the **SELECT** button. A small empty window, like that shown below, will open on the screen. This confirms that the disc is now formatted. The window is empty because as yet there is nothing on the disc. The next chapter deals with filer windows in more detail.

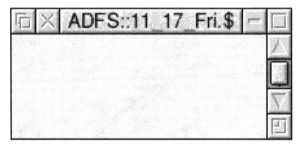

Verifying a disc

It is possible that a disc may report a number of disc errors during the second stage of formatting. This verification process allows you to ensure that there are no serious defects on the disc, which could result in data being lost or corrupted.

If the verification stage (when the **Formatting** window is replaced with a **Verifying** window) reports more than a couple of errors it is best to throw the disc away. A floppy disc only costs a few pence and it really isn't worth risking your data on defective discs.

If you intend you use a disc that has not been recently formatted it is a good idea to verify it to check that it doesn't have any errors before you commit your data to it.

To verify a disc move the mouse pointer over the floppy disc icon and click on **MENU**. The floppy disc menu will now open. Select **Verify** from the menu and a window similar to the Format window will appear and the disc will be verified and any errors found will be reported. As this process is non destructive you can do it to a disc which contains data without affecting the data.

Making a backup copy of a disc.

It is always a good idea to make a *backup* or a copy of any floppy disc that contains valuable data. This also applies to discs used to distribute programs (provided they are not copy protected in some way) just in case the original is lost or damaged.

The easiest way to produce a backup copy of a floppy disc is to place the disc you wish to backup in the drive. Now open the floppy disc menu and click on the **Backup** option with the **SELECT** mouse button.

A window will open inviting you to insert the *Source disc,* and as you've just done that you can click on **OK**. The computer will pause for a few seconds, before starting a process to copy the disc content into memory. Note that if you're copying a disc with more data on it than you have free memory, this process will take several passes.

When prompted to do so, insert the destination disc, and click on **OK**. What you'll be left with is an exact duplicate of the first disc. You can only backup discs of the same size but they do not have to be of the same format type, so 1600K F+ to 1600K F is fine, or 800K D to 800K E is fine, but Acorn 1600K to DOS 1.44M is not as the disc size is very different even though the disc is physically the same.

5. *Filing Systems*

A computer must be able to store and retrieve information. Most users don't need to bother about the technicalities of this, as a user you just need to understand the structure of a normal RISC OS filing system so that you can easily save and load your work where necessary.

RISC OS's 'built in' filing system is called **ADFS** (Advanced Disc Filing System), but a RISC OS computer can actually have several different filing systems. These are normally provided by third parties and can be purely software, such as drivers for parallel port Zip drives, or a combination of hardware and software such as SCSI interfaces. However, these should all work in roughly the same way and so the following information should apply to all of them.

With most current machines it is ADFS that controls the floppy drive, but with some non-Acorn machines the main hard drive may not be controlled by ADFS. For example, with MicroDigital's Omega and Mico computers the hard drive is controlled by their own **IDEFS** , and with the VirtualAcorn emulators the hard disc is controlled by **HostFS** . Don't bother too much about this at this stage. All the information in the following pages applies whatever the actual filing system used as RISC OS is designed to make this sort of thing transparent to the user.

A Filing system has to be able to handle three types of objects;

1. Directories or Folders

2. Files

3. Applications

A simple explanation of each at this stage might be useful.

Directories

Think of a disc as you would think of a filing cabinet; a place to store information. It should have easy access and be well organised and structured so that you can quickly and easily find the items you want.

A floppy disc can contain a lot of information, up to 1.6 megabytes, equivalent to several hundred pages of text, and a hard drive can hold hundreds of gigabytes of data (a gigabyte is normally described as 1000 megabytes, although technically it should be 1024) and this huge amount of information needs to be placed onto the disc in an orderly way so that it can be found when needed.

In a filing cabinet you would normally use dividers to organise the drawer into sections into which you would place appropriate material. Individual papers would then be put into labelled card folders within these section to make it easier to find the specific item you require.

You can create similar divisions and sub-divisions on your discs. We have described these briefly earlier, they are called *Directories* and appear as green folder-shaped icons in the directory viewer window. When you open a directory, the icon will change to that of an open file as an aid to visibility and navigation.

In the same way as you can put several folders into each sub-division of your office filing cabinet, and might even put several associated folders into each of these folders so, with a hard disc, you can have *sub-directories* in each directory, and these sub-directories can, in turn, have their own sub-directories. This is called a *hierarchical filing system*.

As we have seen, to open a viewer on a normal directory you simply double-click on its icon. The directory that opens when you click on a drive icon is known as the *top level* or *root* directory for that drive.

Files

A file is just a piece of data which occupies a location on a disc. It can be almost anything, plain text, a photo, or the output from a program like a spreadsheet or wordprocessor. It can even be a program.

Normally what we refer to as a file is data saved from a program. When a file is saved from a program it will normally be given a specific filetype associated with that program.

Filetypes and their importance under RISC OS will be described later.

Applications

An application is another name for a program, and is contained in a special type of directory called an *Application Directory*. These can be distinguished from ordinary directories because their names all begin with the exclamation character '!'. You can therefore see that you should not use this character when you create a normal directory.

When the '!' character is used as the first character of a name in this way it is pronounced *pling*. So, the **!Boot** directory on your hard drive would be called *"pling boot"*. This might sound a bit strange, but it's a lot quicker and easier to say than *"exclamation mark boot"*.

To run a program you just double-click on its application directory.

Application directories don't have the usual folder icon. They will have a specific icon to represents the program pictorially. Usually a variation of this icon will be used for files associated with the program, and, when you run the program, a similar icon will be used on the icon bar.

Opening an application directory

Application directories are created when you install the program, so you would not normally need to do anything inside them. However, there are times when this may be necessary, and you will have realised that, since double-clicking on an application directory runs the program. they can't be opened like normal directories.

To open an application directory simply hold down either of the **Shift** keys when you double-click on it.

Examining your hard disc structure

The following section assumes that you have a standard hard drive build as installed on a new computer. If your machine is not new or was purchased secondhand then you might have additional directories and applications or some of those described may not be present.

Click **SELECT** on the hard disc drive icon HardDisc4 to open the filer window. You are now looking at the *Root* directory - the top of the branching structure which is why it is also known sometimes called the *Top Level directory*.

Application

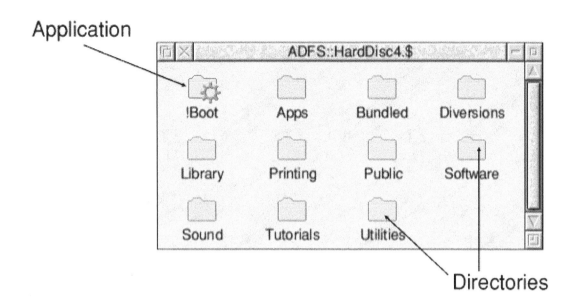

ADFS::HardDisc4.$

!Boot   Apps   Bundled   Diversions

Library   Printing   Public   Software

Sound   Tutorials   Utilities

Directories

The title bar of a directory viewer always shows the full pathname of the directory you are looking at. If you have a standard RISC OS computer the title bar would typically show: **ADFS::HardDisc4.$**

The first part of the name, up to the two '::' characters, is the filing system name, in this case ADFS. As we have already said, you can have more than one filing system on a RISC OS computer, so the complete pathname of a file or directory always begins with the name of the filing system.

After this is the name of the actual disc, in this case HardDisc4.

RISC OS doesn't use drive numbers or letters in the same way as a PC, it gives discs and drives names instead. The '4' in the name is not important. Drives *are* allocated numbers, we have already seen that the floppy drive is actually drive '0' on ADFS, but you should not need to worry about them in normal use.

The last part of the name is the '$' (dollar) symbol. This is a special character that is used to represent the root directory of the disc, which is what we are looking at.

There is one application in the window called **!Boot**. This is a special application that contains certain components required to let RISC OS run properly. It also sets up any external devices and installs any software that you want to be run at switch on. Its place at the root of the hard drive ensures that it's seen before anything else. All the other items in this window are normal directories.

Move the mouse pointer over the directory **Tutorials** and double-click **SELECT**. This will open the directory **Tutorials**. Look at the title bar of this window, you can see that the title of the directory is an extension of the title of the previous window, in other words you have moved one level down the tree structure. In this new window you should see three directories; **DrawTutor, PaintTutor** and **WelcomeGuide** with two text files, **ReadMe** and **StarComms**.

Double-click **SELECT** on the directory **DrawTutor** and you will open another window, the third level of the directory structure, and once again the title bar of the window will show this.

You can therefore see that the filing system is laid out like an upside down tree. At the 'top' of the structure is the **Root** ($) directory and this divides into **sub-directories,** which may again divide with further **sub-directories,** and so on.

At each level of the structure you can place files, directories or applications. The only limitations are the physical capacity of your disc, and the length of the filename - your filenames can have a maximum of 255 characters, which should be enough for most of us.

6. The Filer

••

The Filer is the system that lets you access the features of the Filing System, in other words, to move around the RISC OS directory structure, to load and save files, run programs and carry out various other operations on files.

Filer Menu

The filer menu appears each time you click the **MENU** button when the pointer is over a directory viewer or window. An example filer menu is shown below. This is the result of clicking **MENU** while the mouse pointer was over the icon for a Text file called "ReadMe".

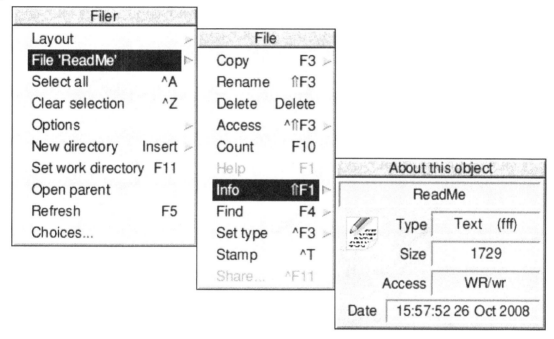

The filer menu will always contain the same items, but sometimes one or more of these will appear in grey instead of black. A grey menu option cannot be selected, and this means that the option is inappropriate at that stage. For example, if you click the HardDisc4 icon then click the **MENU** button while the root directory is open the *Open Parent* option will be "greyed out" as you are already viewing the top level directory so there is no parent.

The rest of this chapter describes the various items on the filer menu and its sub-menus.

Layout

This lets you change the way the directory viewer displays the contents of a directory. Move the mouse over the arrow to the right of Layout and onto the Layout window. You will see something similar to the picture below.

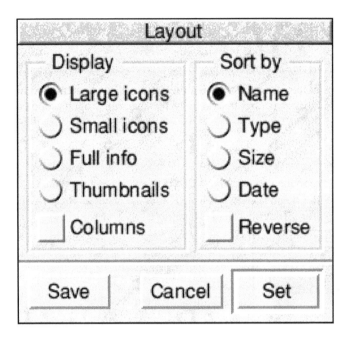

Large icons means that the display is shown, as in the previous illustrations, with full size icons and the name below the icon.

Small icons, as the name suggests, uses half size icons for folders, applications and files with the name beside the icon instead of below it. This is more compact so you can see more of the contents of a directory if it contains a large number of objects.

Full info shows the contents in a single vertical column with small icons. To the right of each icon is not just the filename but also information about the file, its type, size, access status and the date it was created or last modified as shown.

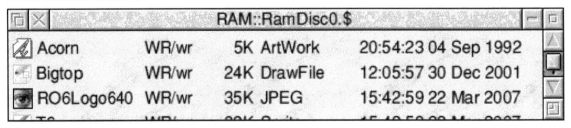

Thumbnails will display a thumbnail image of each file. A thumbnail is a small image of the file concerned. For example selecting the **Thumbnails** option will show small sized samples of any graphics files, these include Sprites, Drawfiles, JPEGs, GIFs etc. Files that do not have an image in them will be displayed with their normal large icon.

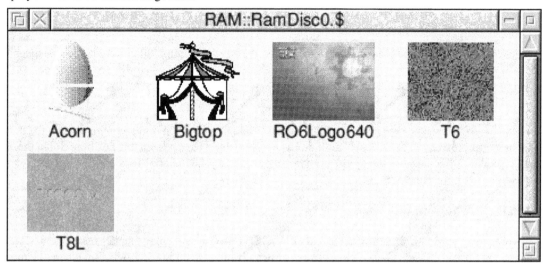

Columns will display your files sequenced down columns rather than across rows as was the original behaviour. In Column mode, the vertical scroll bar is replaced with a horizontal one instead.

In addition to the type of display, there are five options which define how the items in the window are sorted.

Sort by name will sort the items in a directory alphabetically, whatever their type.

Sort by type will sort all the objects by filetype. Note that they are sorted by their filetype number, not name, (more about this later) so may not appear in the order you would expect. Within each group of items of the same type files will be sorted alphabetically.

Sort by size will, as you might expect, sort files by their size, the largest file first.

Sort by date will sort the files by the date they were created or last modified. The latest appearing first, at the top of the filer window.

Reverse will sort the files by the method chosen from one of the four options above, but will do so in reverse order.

You can experiment with these options and see how the filer display changes.

With older versions of RISC OS, changes made here became permanent and so would apply the next time you switch on. With RISC OS Six and above the permanent changes are set in the main Configure program, which will be described later. Changes made from these menus only remain in force until you switch off.

The one slight exception to the above, with version 6.12 or later, is that there is now the option to configure layout permanence. With permanent layouts enabled (see the Configure section of this guide), the **Save** button on the Layout window will save the selected layout options for the directory over which the Filer menu was opened. This saved layout will override, for the directory in question, any other defaults or automatic layouts.

To delete a saved layout, deselect all icons in this layout window (using **ADJUST** on the Radio icons) and click **Save.**

Selection

This is the option below **Layout** on the filer menu. It actually shows which objects the action you are intending to perform will be carried out on, so precisely what appears in this position depends upon where the mouse was when you clicked the **MENU** button and whether any items in the window had been selected.

If you had previously selected two or more objects, then the word **Selection** will appear here. This means that whatever you intend to do will be done to all of the selected objects. As you will see later some operations can only be carried out on single files, and so if you have selected more than one object these items will be grey on their respective menus so that they can't be used.

If no items were selected and the mouse pointer was over a file, application or directory icon then the name of that item (preceded by "File", "App." or "Dir." as appropriate) will appear in this position. So, in the example shown earlier, because the mouse pointer was over a Text file named "ReadMe" what appeared in this position was **File "ReadMe"**.

The Selection sub-menu

Open a directory viewer on your hard drive and click **MENU** over it to display the filer menu. Now slide off the second item on the menu, (which could say any of a variety of things depending on where the mouse pointer was when you clicked **MENU** , as described previously) to open the **Selection** menu, which will look something like the one on the right.

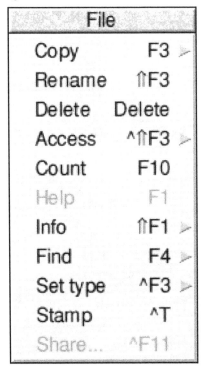

With your hard drive filer window open (displaying something like ADFS::HardDisc4.$ at the top), click on the **Apps** directory - the directory will become highlighted. Click the **MENU** button and you will see that the Selection option shows **"Dir. Apps"** . Moving the mouse to the right over the arrow will take you into the directory sub-menu. If you select any option within this menu it will be carried out on the directory Apps.

The options on this sub-menu are:

- **Copy** - Lets you make an exact copy of the selected object. Copying is described fully later.

- **Rename** - This lets you change the name of the item you have just selected. Enter a new name into the field provided, then press the **Return** or **Enter** key. You should also see the section in Chapter 8 on renaming.

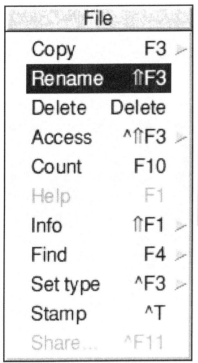

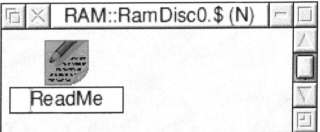

- **Delete** - Delete the item currently selected. Use this with care, if you delete a directory you will delete all its contents and any sub-directories with their contents. Once an item has been deleted there is normally no way to recover it. However if you have the RISC OS Six Recycle bin (Recyclone) activated then your file will be moved into the recycle bin so it can be recovered if you have made a mistake.

- **Access** - Lets you set or unset the attributes protecting the file from deletion or allowing deletion and also whether the file can be seen across a network. These will be described later.

- **Count** - Displays the size of the file if the current selection is a file or, if it's a directory, the sum of the sizes of all the files in the directory and the files in any sub-directories.

- **Help** - If you have selected an application directory the Help option allows you to view any help data contained within it.
  Note that not all applications are supplied with Help files, and will often require you to refer to alternative documentation.

- **Info** - Displays information about the file or folder currently selected, including its type, size, access rights and the date it was created or last updated.

- **Find** - Lets you search for a filename, or part of a filename, within the currently selected directory.

- **Set Type** - Lets you apply a RISC OS file type to the selected file. This can be useful with material originating on other machines as you may need to set its filetype to ensure that RISC OS can identify it. Obviously this option can't be used with directories.

- **Stamp** - Forces the current date and time onto the currently selected file or directory. This can come in useful if you wish to keep track of the dates on which files were copied onto your computer.

- **Share** this allows a folder (or directory) to be shared across a RISC OS network. This option will be greyed out unless you have a folder selected when you press on **MENU** to open the filer menu. If you click on the **Share...** option then the following window will be opened:

From here you can control how the folder, and hence its contents, are shared across your network. You can make the folder available as "read only" so that the contents cannot be altered by other users on other machines. You can share items as "CD-Roms" and you can also set up a password so that only other users on the network who have the password can access the files.

Some operations can be carried out on more than one item if several are selected and many of the options above are available for both files and folders. Obviously not all operations can be performed on a group of objects, for example, you can't rename a group of files.

Select all

As you might expect this selects all the objects in the directory.

Clear selection

De-selects any and all objects that have been selected.

Options

This leads to a menu that lets you set a number of options that affect the way filer operations are carried out.

The Options sub menu

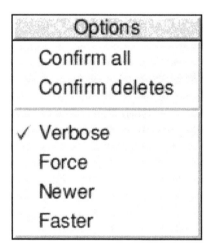

- **Confirm All** - If this is selected then whenever you carry out an operation on a file such as copying, moving, deleting, etc. a window will open asking you to confirm that you want this to happen. This would normally be switched off.

- **Confirm Deletes** - If this is selected then whenever you try to delete an object a window will open asking you to confirm that you really do want to delete it. New users might prefer to have it on until they become more familiar with RISC OS to avoid accidentally deleting something that they didn't really intend to. However, repeatedly confirming that you do want to delete things can get very tedious, which is why most people have this option switched off.

- **Verbose** - If this is on then when you carry out any operation on a file or files a filer action window will open displaying progress.

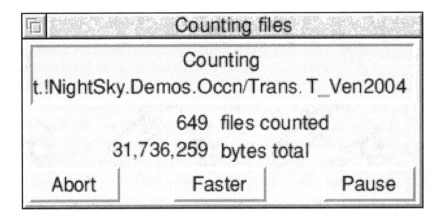

- **Force** - As you will see later files can be locked to prevent them from being accidentally deleted. Normally if you try to delete or overwrite a locked file you won't be able to do so, you will just get an error message telling you that the file is locked.
  If Force is on then locked files will be deleted or overwritten without any warning. There may be times when this option could be used but you are strongly advised to set it to 'Off'.

- **Newer** - Normally if you save, move or copy a file into a directory where there is already a file of the same name the new file will overwrite and replace the old. If **Newer** is switched on then this will only happen if the new file has a later date than the old, that is, it actually *is* a newer file. This can prevent accidentally replacing a later version of, say, a DTP document with an older version.

- **Faster** - When carrying out operations on files RISC OS normally multi-tasks so that you can carry on with other work and, if Verbose is enabled, as it normally would be, you can see this in the Filer Action window. If Faster is *On* then, although there is still a limited amount of multi-tasking, the filer takes precedent, full information about what is happening is not displayed in the Filer Action window and anything else you are trying to do at the same time will be very slow. However the file operations will be quicker, which is useful if, for example, you are copying a lot of files. You will notice a button labelled **Faster** in the Filer Action window. This has exactly the same effect and lets you switch to Faster mode temporarily to speed up protracted filer operations

As with the Display options described earlier options selected from this menu only remain in force until you switch off the computer. They can be set permanently using the Configure application described later.

New Directory

This lets you create a new directory or folder. You will find as you acquire more files and applications that you need to create directories to put them in. Try to do this in a methodical way so that you can group similar items together to help you to find them when you need them just as you do with a 'paper' filing system.

When you choose a name for a directory it is a good idea to make it reflect the contents, e.g. Letters, Games etc. There are a few restrictions on the characters you can use in directory names;

- Directory names are best kept short. RISC OS Six allows up to 255 characters in file or directory names but you normally only see about the first fifteen letters in the display. Also if you use directory names that are more than about a dozen characters long then the full pathname, if the directories are 'nested' deeply, can become too long for some older programs to cope with.

- Never use the ! symbol as the first in a directory name. This will make RISC OS think it's an application directory. There are other characters that you shouldn't use and these are listed in the next chapter in the section on copying files.

- Avoid using punctuation marks in directory or file names. Although some of these are allowed they aren't permitted on some other disc formats, for example, if you want to copy a file to a DOS floppy disc, and they can also cause problems with some programs.

- Ideally use a name which does not already exist on your drive to avoid confusion.

Open the Filer menu and slide the mouse pointer off *New Directory* and the window shown will appear.

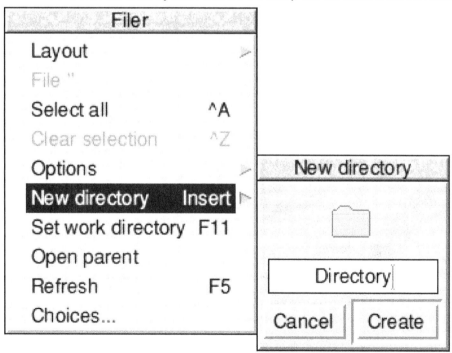

A default name of 'Directory' is placed in the icon for the new directory name. You probably won't want to use this, so delete it using the **Backspace** key and enter the name of your choice.

If you now either press the **Return** key or click on the **OK** button the new directory will be created in the same directory that the mouse pointer was over when you opened the Filer menu.

Alternatively you can drag the folder icon in the window to a directory viewer and the new directory will be created there. To drag the icon just put the mouse pointer over it and hold down the **SELECT** button. Move the mouse pointer while keeping **SELECT** held down and the Folder icon will follow. When it is over the directory viewer you want to create the new directory in just release the mouse button.

With recent versions of the Filer, it is possible to create a directory structure in one single operation, by giving a pathname with dots separating the subdirectories, for example **a.b.c.d**. If any part of that path does not exist, Filer will create it as necessary.

Set work directory

This makes the directory the mouse pointer was over when you opened the Filer menu the *Currently Selected Directory* (CSD). There is no need to bother too much about this as you will probably never need to use this facility.

Open Parent

As you might expect this will open the parent directory of the directory the mouse pointer was over when you opened the Filer menu. It is similar to clicking **ADJUST** on the window's close icon except that it leaves the first directory viewer open.

Refresh

This re-reads the contents of a directory from the filing system and updates the display. It can be useful if a filing system does not notify the filer about changes to the directory contents.

Keyboard shortcuts

Keyboard shortcuts for Filer were first introduced in RISC OS 6.06, later versions expand on those and provide greater power and flexibility when using the keyboard. Since Filer is now able to display vertical (column) layout or the normal horizontal (row) layout of objects in a viewer, some keyboard shortcuts have alternate behaviour according to which view layout is active. These are the shortcuts which have meanings with "or" in their descriptions.

Below are the standard keyboard shortcuts for Filer that will allow you to navigate around viewers and load files and applications from the keyboard.

Key	Meaning
^Insert	Toggle viewer retention behaviour (see -RetainViewer)
Tab	Move the focus to the next viewer
Shift-Tab	Move the focus to the previous viewer
^	Open current viewers parent with focus
$	Open current viewers root with focus
Page Up	Move one window full up, or one window full right
Page Down	Move one window full down, or one window full left
Up	Move the highlight up one
Down	Move the highlight down one
Left	Move the highlight left one
Right	Move the highlight right one

^Up	Move the highlight to the first object, or top of column
^Down	Move the highlight to the last object, or bottom of column
^Left	Move the highlight to the left of row, or to the first object
^Right	Move the highlight to the right of row, or to the last object

The following shortcuts are used when building a selection of files. These will be easier to understand if you experiment in Filer whilst reading them.

Key	Meaning
^[Shift]-A	Select all objects in the current viewer
^[Shift]-Z	Clear the current selection
^[Shift]-Space	Toggle the selection of the highlight object
^Shift-Tab	Swap active selection end points
^Shift-Left	Toggle select left one object, or left up one column
^Shift-Right	Toggle select right one object, or right down one column
^Shift-Up	Toggle select left up one row, or up one object
^Shift-Down	Toggle select right down one row, or down one object

There are a number of keyboard shortcuts which will perform actions previously only possible with the mouse and menus, these are listed in the following table.

Key	Meaning
Escape	Cancel drag or key selection
Return	Perform the 'run' action on selected object(s) in current viewer, either running files or opening directories.
Shift-Return	Perform alternate action on the selected object(s): Load files into a text editor Close open directories, or open a new directory Open applications
Insert	Create a new directory (path) in the current viewer
Delete	Delete selected object(s) after confirmation
Shift-Delete	Delete selected object(s)
^T	Timestamp selected object(s) in current viewer
F1	Load help for selected application (if available)
Shift-F1	Info on selected object
F2	Force selected image(s) to be [re-]thumbnailed (Thumbnail mode only).
^F2	Close the current viewer
F3	Copy selected object in current viewer
Shift-F3	Rename selected object(s)
^F3	Set type of selected object(s)

^Shift-F3	Set access for selected object(s)
F4	Find object within selected object(s) in current viewer
F5	Refresh the current viewer
F6	Cycle through sort orders for the current viewer
Shift-F6	Reverse cycle through sort orders
^F6	Toggle reverse sort order
F7	Cycle through display formats for the current viewer
Shift-F7	Reverse cycle through display formats
^F7	Toggle display orientation
F10	Count selected object(s) in current viewer
F11	Set work directory to the current viewer
^F11	Share selected directory

Alphanumeric keys: These move the highlight through the files as the name is progressively entered. The break for typing the name of the object is 1 second. Any keys pressed after this will initiate a new search.

Notes

It is strongly advised that Recyclone is used with key shortcuts, although some limited protection has been added to the Delete key shortcut.

- Delete will always prompt for confirmation, regardless of configuration.

- Shift-Delete will only ask for confirmation if configured to do so.

- ^Shift-Delete does nothing, intentionally.

Refresh (F5) now also re-evaluates -AutoThumb ratio (if enabled) and forces images which were previously too big to be re-tried (for thumbnail display).

Search as you type will move to the nearest object for 'sort by name'. For other sort types the highlight will move only when an exact match is found. If you wish to search for an object name that starts with a Space character you must press Space twice. This is not required for a Space within a name.

The 'new directory', 'copy as', and 'rename' writables can now contain a sub-path. A sub-path is created (relative to the viewer directory) if it does not exist, raising an error if any part already exists but is not a directory.

Filer toolbars

Filer now has support for toolbars. This feature allows users to add their own toolbars or those published by others, to Filer. Below is a picture of Filer with a toolbar at the top.

7. Copy, Moving and Renaming Files

There will be many occasions when you wish to make a copy of a file. You might need to do this for security reasons, keeping a copy in case your original is accidentally deleted or the disc is damaged, etc. or you may want to make a copy of a document before you make alterations to it so that you can revert to the previous version if necessary.

This chapter will describe the actions to copy a single file or group of files but the procedures are exactly the same for copying a folder or group of folders.

Copying within a directory

As previously described this option is found on the **Selection** sub-menu of the Filer menu. You must use this method to copy within a directory as this is the only way you can give a different name to the copy. You must do this when copying in the same directory since you can't have two files or directories (or a file and a directory) with the same name in a directory.

Begin by either selecting the file or folder you want to copy or placing the mouse pointer over the object you want to copy when you press **MENU** to open the Filer menu. Because you must rename objects when copying in the same directory and you can only rename one object at a time if more than one object is selected when you open the Filer menu you will find that the **Copy** option is feint and can't be used.

Assuming that you have only selected a single object slide the mouse pointer off Copy on the Selection sub-menu to open the Copy window. This is similar to the New Directory window previously described and you use it in a similar way.

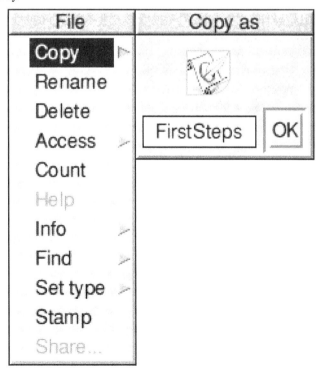

The name of the selected file or directory will appear in the Copy window. You will need to alter this or delete this name and enter a completely new name. When you have done this either press the **Return** key or click on the '**OK** ' button and the file or directory will be copied.

With a file this will probably be very quick, unless it's a very large file, but if you are copying a directory the operation may take some considerable time, especially if it contains a large number of files. During this operation a Filer Action window will open (unless *Verbose* has been set Off) to display progress, although if you are copying just a single file its appearance may be so brief as to be almost unnoticeable.

Copying between directories

You will almost certainly find that you need to do this much more often than copying within the same directory. The easiest way to copy objects to another directory is by dragging. The destination directory can be a different directory on the same drive or on a completely different drive, for example, copying from a floppy drive to a hard drive or visa versa.

The following exercise will illustrate this.

1. Click with **SELECT** on the hard disc icon to open a directory viewer onto the root directory of your hard drive.

2. Double-click with **SELECT** on the **Tutorials** folder to open that.

3. Drag this new window to one side so that it is not obscuring the first window. You should now be able to see the two windows, The **HardDisc4** root directory window and the **Tutorials** directory window.

4. Move the pointer over the file **ReadMe** in the **Tutorials** directory and click and hold down the **SELECT** button. The file icon will become selected and inverted in colour. Now drag the file icon into the **HardDisc4** directory and release the mouse button.

5. The file will be copied as soon as you release the mouse button. It does not matter exactly where the pointer is when you release the button, as long as it is somewhere over the window you wish to copy into. If the Filer is currently set to *Sort by name* the file will be slotted in alphabetically. You now have a second copy of the ReadMe file.

Copying multiple files

Using the method described above you are not restricted to copying one file at a time. If you select a group of files or directories or a mixture of both then they will all be copied.

Select all the files or directories you want to copy by any of the methods described in Chapter 3. Now place the mouse pointer over any of these selected objects and click and hold down the **ADJUST** button and drag it to the destination directory. All the selected objects will be copied.

Note that you must use the **ADJUST** button for this to work properly, not **SELECT**. If you try to use **SELECT** then, as we have already seen, the object the mouse pointer is over when the button was pressed will be selected and all the others will be de-selected, so only that single object would be copied.

Renaming while copying

When you drag a file or directory to copy it the copy will have the same name as the original. There may be times when you want to give the copy a new name. For example, if you were writing a book the original might be called *MyBook* but you might want to keep backup copies at various stages called, say, *MyBook1, MyBook2, MyBook3*, etc.

You can use a variation of the method used to copy within a directory to simultaneously copy and rename a file or directory.

Open a directory viewer for the directory you want to copy so that you have both source and destination directories visible. Now use the method described in **Copying within a directory** but, after changing the name, don't press the **Return** key or click on '**OK**'.

You will see an icon in the centre of the window. This will be the same as the icon for the file or application you are copying or, if it's a directory, it will be the folder icon. Drag this icon to the destination directory viewer and the object will be copied.

Obviously you can only copy items one at a time using this method.

When you copy directories using this method only the name of the directory you are actually copying will be changed, the contents remain the same.

Moving Files

The procedure for moving files is almost identical to copying by dragging but with one important difference. Before you hold down the **SELECT** or **ADJUST** button on the mouse, with your other hand press and hold down either of the **Shift** keys on the keyboard.

Now drag the object or objects just as if you were copying them, but if you keep the **Shift** key held down while you drag them you will find that the files will appear in the destination directory but will have vanished from the source directory; that is, they have been *moved* instead of *copied*.

If you are moving files between directories on the same drive this will be very fast. Even if you are moving a directory containing a lot of large files it will still be extremely rapid. This is because the actual files on the drive aren't physically moved to the new location, it's only necessary to re-arrange some of the information that describes where they appear in the directory structure.

If you are moving data between drives then it will be a lot slower. This is because the filer then has to actually copy each file in turn to the new location, then delete the original. Obviously this takes a lot more time, slightly longer than copying.

Warning

While you are carrying out any copy or move operations or any other operations which involve writing to the hard drive it is very important that you do not switch the computer off.

It is good practice to always use the proper Shutdown procedure before switching off any computer. If you switch off while file operations are being carried out there is a very high risk that some of the data on your hard drive could become 'scrambled' making the drive unreadable.

This won't permanently damage the drive, but you could have lost all your files and data forever.

Never move the computer while the drive is being read from or written to. It's a good idea not to move it while it's switched on anyway, but if the computer is jarred or shaken while the hard drive is in use it is possible for the read/write head to make contact with the drive platter. This can result in permanent damage.

Renaming

Earlier the use of **Rename** on the **Selection** sub-menu of the Filer menu was described. Previously this was the only way of renaming files or directories. From RISC OS 4 onwards a much simpler method can also be used:

To rename a file or directory place the mouse pointer over its name (not the icon itself) in a Filer window and click **SELECT** while holding down either **Alt** key. You'll find these keys at either end of the spacebar. The area in the Filer window where the name was will now change into a writable icon as shown below. Alter the name in the icon, then press **Return** and the name will be changed.

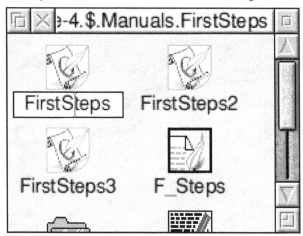

It is also possible to initiate the renaming operation using the **Shift+F3** keyboard shortcut if these are enabled.

If you make a mistake and don't want the name to change then press **Escape** or click the mouse anywhere else in the filer window. The rename icon will vanish leaving the original name unaltered.

Advanced renaming features

RISC OS now has some powerful ways to rename your files. Multiple selected files can be renamed in quick succession by use of **Shift + Enter** rather than just the **Enter** key to complete each rename. To do this, select several files or directories and use the **Alt** key and **SELECT** mouse button on the first one as normal, then just use **Alt + Enter** to move to the next file to be renamed. Files are deselected as you go, until there are no more to be renamed.

Another powerful rename feature now available is that of changing the location of a file at the same time as renaming it. By including special directory path characters in its new name, you can instruct Filer to relocate the file into another part of the file system relative to the current location.

The ^ character (found on the **6** key on UK keyboards) is used by RISC OS filing systems to mean, up one directory. The **.** (fullstop) character is a directory separator. Using these characters you can specify a relative path when renaming. If the new path does not exist, Filer creates it.

As an example, you could specify a new name for a file as ^.^.a.b.RISCOS6. This would mean go up two levels from the current directory then go into a directory called a, and inside that, one called b and put the new file called file RISCOS6 in there. The old file would disappear as it moved and if necessary, the new directory path would be created.

Illegal characters in filenames

There are some reserved characters that you cannot use in RISC OS file or directory names. Most of these are not permitted because they have some 'special meaning'. For example, we have already said that you should not use '!' as the first character of a directory name as RISC OS assumes that any directory name beginning with '!' is an application directory.

The following characters are not allowed -

`$, %, &, *, #, @, ", |, ^,` and the full stop '.' and colon ':'

You can't use a "normal" space character in a file or directory name. However you can use what is known as an **Alt Space**. This is the character that you would get on screen if you held down **ALT** and pressed **Space** in an Edit window. This produces ASCII character 160 instead of 32 (the 'normal' space) and as this character is defined as a blank in most fonts it will still look like a space but, since it actually isn't one, it's permitted. RISC OS Six does this for you automatically if you type a 'normal' space when creating or renaming a file, but many applications won't permit a space to be used when saving files, so you will then need to use **Alt-Space**.

It is also best not to use the forward slash '/' character as although this isn't forbidden it has a special meaning described below.

It is bad practice (and ugly) to use all upper case names. In case 'ugly' and 'difficult to read' aren't enough there is also a practical reason. With most fonts, especially the default Homerton, upper case letters are a lot bigger than lower case, so names are longer and even quite short names may be too long to fit in the space allocated in a filer window. This means that the end of the name might not be visible. For example -

LatestVersion
LATESTVERSION

but the all upper case name might appear as - LATESTVERS

even if the mixed case version fitted in the space provided with room to spare.

Transferring files to other systems

As we said earlier RISC OS identifies files by their *Filetype* . This is specific to Acorn format discs, and most other operating systems, including CD ROMs, use a system known as the *Dot Extension*. This means that after the descriptive name of the file there is a full stop (the 'dot') and then a three (now sometimes four or more) letter extension which defines what type of file it is.

Some extensions are specific to particular programs but many of them are more general, such as TXT for a plain text file, JPG for a Jpeg graphic image, ZIP for a compressed Zip file, and so on.

Since the full stop is not allowed in RISC OS filenames there has to be another way of representing these extensions. This is done by substituting the '/' (forward slash) character. This means that if you are looking at a CD ROM or DOS format disc in a filer window you would see 'README/TXT' instead of 'README.TXT'.

RISC OS has a module called *MimeMap* which, when it sees a file on a CD ROM or DOS format disc with an extension that it 'knows' about, displays it with an equivalent RISC OS filetype icon, thus making it much easier to identify the type of file.

If you want to transfer a file to a computer running another operating system, for example, Windows, you can do so on a DOS formatted floppy disc, but you would need to add the appropriate extension, using '/' instead of a full stop. If you don't do this then the other machine won't know what type of file it is.

8. *Using Filetypes*

We have previously mentioned Filetypes, and this is a very important part of the way that RISC OS operates.

With most operating systems, to make a program load a certain file when you double-click on it you have to *associate* that type of file with a particular program. This normally means adding it to a list kept by the operating system. If you remove that program or move it elsewhere on your hard drive or install another program that you would prefer to load that type of file you have to alter the list.

With RISC OS it is the program itself that declares what type of file it wants to load when you double-click on it by setting a *Load Alias* and, if clicking on the file should also run the program if it's not running already, it will set a *Run Alias* for the file. The program also provides the sprites for the files. This is all done by the !Boot file within the application directory, and as soon as the filer sees an application for the first time it will obey the instructions in the !Boot file and set up the necessary aliases.

It therefore doesn't matter where on your hard drive the program is, or even which drive it's on. As long as the filer has 'seen' the program it will set any required aliases and load the sprites for the program's files so that files of that type will be displayed correctly.

Filetypes consist of a three digit hexadecimal number, but for most common types there is also an associated name, so the filetype can be referred to, or have its type set, either by its number or name.

Shown below are two windows produced from **Info** on the Filer menu. One is for a DrawFile, the other for a plain text file. In both cases the Info window shows the filetype name, its number, and the sprite associated with that type of file. As you become familiar with RISC OS you will learn to recognise many of these file types.

 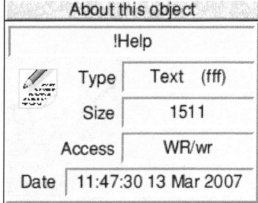

Introduced in RISC OS 6.10 is a new way to set the type of files using a list of currently known types, instead of the user having to know the exact name or number of a type. Below is a picture of the new menu.

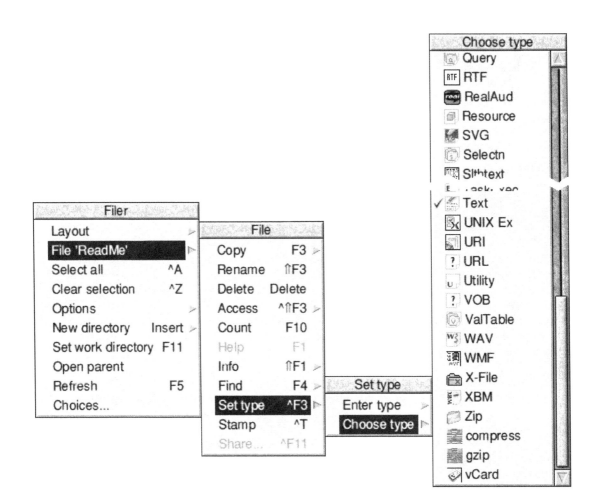

9. The Task Manager

RISC OS incorporates a comprehensive means of allowing the user to keep track of all the various programs or **Tasks** that are running and the memory they are using. All of this information is displayed in the **Task Manager** window.

This is more than just a display of what's going on, you can also use it to make alterations to some items.

Click the **MENU** button with the mouse pointer over the rightmost icon on the icon bar (shown left) and the menu shown will appear. For standard RISC OS Six this icon will be in the form of the RISC OS Six 'Cog', for earlier versions of RISC OS the icon may be different but it will always be the icon at the extreme right hand end of the icon bar.

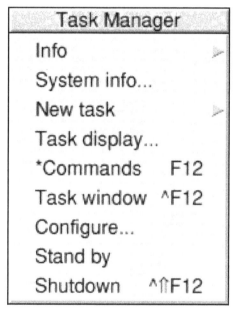

- **Info** - If you slide off this item to the right a window will open giving you more information about the version of RISC OS that you are using. You will find that most RISC OS programs have a similar 'Info' window available from their icon bar menu.

- **System info** - This opens a window showing graphical representations of memory allocation at the time the menu was clicked.

- **New task** - You will probably never need to use this. It is simply a method of executing an OS or 'star' command without either leaving the desktop or opening a Task Window.

- **Task Display** - We'll come to this soon.

- ***Commands** - This is equivalent to pressing **F12** as previously described at the end of Chapter 1.

- **Task Window** - As you might expect this will open a Task Window equivalent to pressing **Ctrl-F12**.

- **Configure** - This will open the RISC OS configuration system, in a similar way to double clicking on !Boot.

- **Stand by** - If your machine supports power saving then this will put the computer into power saving mode.

- **Shutdown** - This will shut down the computer, the same as pressing **Shift-Ctrl-F12**

System info

The System information window uses the RISC OS 6 DrawChart feature to display memory usage in graphical pie charts. This helps you see at a glance where memory has been used.

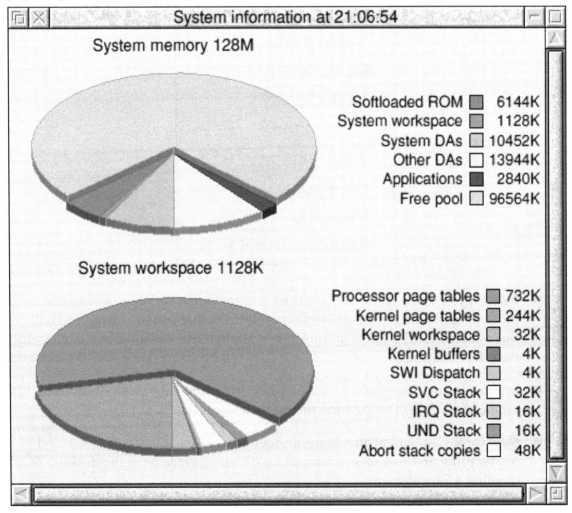

The charts show a snap-shot of the usage at the time the display was opened.

The Task Display

You can open the Task Display window by selecting that option from the menu or by clicking on the Task Manager icon with **SELECT**. This will open a window similar to the one below.

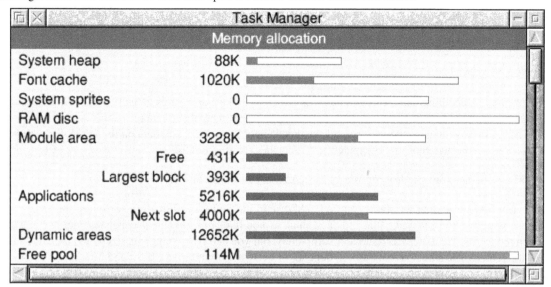

Upon initial opening of the Task display window, its size will default to the top section only. This top section shows a summary of memory usage across the different memory areas of the system. The information is shown both in figures and graphically by the coloured sliders.

Red sliders may be changed by dragging them with the mouse left or right to decrease or increase the allocated memory. The solid colour part of the sliders shows the current usage, whereas the white area indicates the maximum possible allocation of memory to that area.

Of those areas which are user draggable, the most likely ones you will change are:

- **Font cache**

- **RAM disc**

- **Next slot**

These are described in more detail below.

The dark green bars show information about used memory in the different areas. These will change as memory allocation changes, but are not user draggable.

At the top of the list of memory areas is an area that shows the **System heap** memory usage, that is, the memory used by all the various components of RISC OS itself. Although this is user draggable, it is unlikely you will need to modify this. RISC OS will increase the memory allocated as and when it needs to, although you may find that you can sometimes recover memory back to the free pool by dragging this slider left if you've been working with lots of resources and then later tidied up by closing programs and files afterwards. If you're unsure what you are doing, do not modify this.

Font cache is the amount of memory reserved for caching or 'remembering' fonts. If this is too small and you are viewing something like a DTP document that uses a large number of different fonts RISC OS won't be able to cache all the fonts and so will have to keep loading them from disc. This is very much slower than loading the fonts from a font cache held in memory, so viewing the document will be slow and jerky.

If this happens then try dragging the Font cache slider to the right to allocate more memory.

System sprites is an area not normally used by modern RISC OS programs, so it would normally be set to zero by default. However, some very old programs may need some memory to be allocated in this area. There are ways that a program can do this itself, but if you get an error message saying something like 'Not enough room in System sprites area' when you run an old program you could try dragging this slider out to allocate some memory.

The RAM disc

A RAM disc is something that looks and behaves like a small hard disc but is actually located in the computer's memory instead of on some type of physical media. The big advantage of this is that it is very fast. The big disadvantage is that because all the data is held in memory any data on the RAM disc will be lost as soon as you switch off the computer or if it crashes for any reason.

A RAM disc is therefore an ideal repository for temporary or transient files.

To create a RAM disc drag the slider next to RAM disc in the **Memory allocation** section of the Task Manager window. You can make it as big or as small as you like, and you can alter its size later if you wish, or even reduce its size to zero to remove it completely, but you can *only* change its size when there are no files stored on it. The size you make it will depend on what you intend to use it for and how much memory is installed in your computer, but around 4 Mb would probably be enough for most purposes.

When you drag the RAM disc slider to the right this creates a RAM disc. You will see that a new icon has appeared on the icon bar to the left of the Apps icon. This is the RAM disc icon, and you can click on it to open a filer window onto the RAM disc just as you can with any other drive.

If you have some files stored on a RAM disc when you shut the computer down then you will be warned and given the option of aborting the shutdown in case some of the files are wanted. Don't forget that any files left on a RAM disc when you shut down will be lost forever.

Module area (sometimes called RMA) is a special area of memory in which Relocatable Modules are loaded and executed. This area can grow as required, but it can only shrink if the free space within it is at the end of the area. For this reason, **Module area** also keeps track of the blocks of free space within and tries to use these efficiently when new modules are loaded.

The dark green **Free** and **Largest block** sliders indicate how fragmented the **RMA** is. If the **Free** slider is large, it is quite possible that some of the free space in the **RMA** is at the end of the area and it may be possible to recover some memory back to the **Free pool** by dragging the slider for **Module area** to the left.

The **Applications** slider shows how much of the computer's memory is in use by all the running applications. More detail about the applications that are running is available in the **Tasks** section of the window.

Next slot is the amount of RAM that will be allocated by default to the next task that starts up. Usually when a program starts it tells RISC OS how much RAM it needs and that is the amount that will be allocated, but not all programs do this. If a program doesn't ask for a specific amount of RAM then the amount set in **Next slot** will be given to it.

Dynamic areas shows the total memory in use by all dynamic areas. These are listed individually in the last section of the task display window.

Free pool gives the total amound of unallocated memory that is free for allocation to any of the other areas and is therefore shown in a different colour to illustrate that it is unallocated.

The next section of the window is **Tasks**.The size of this section changes according to how many tasks are running. The picture below shows some of the tasks that were running on the computer used to write this guide.

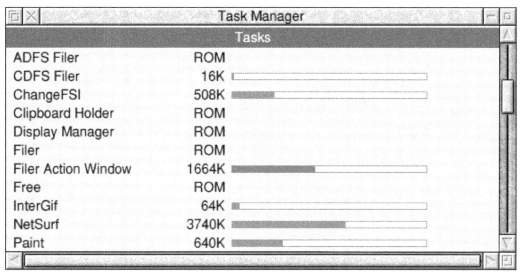

The **Tasks** section shows all the running tasks in the system and whether they're running from ROM, or are using either application memory or RMA memory. Tasks using application memory will have a slider displaying how much memory they are using, in addition to the memory in figures.

Note that Tasks are now listed in alphabetical order rather than in the order they were started. More tasks would be visible if this example window were to be scrolled or enlarged.

To see how the Tasks display works, with the Task Manager window open press **Ctrl-F12** to open a Task Window. This may open over the Task Manager window so drag it out of the way and you will see that a new Task has appeared on the list called *TaskWindow* using the amount of RAM that is set in the red **Next slot** entry in the **Memory allocation** section at the top of the window. Close the Task Window. You will find that if you click and hold down **SELECT** with the mouse pointer near the right hand end of the **Next slot** slider you can drag this slider to the left or right, increasing or decreasing the amount of memory that will be allocated to the next task. Once you have altered the amount press **Ctrl-F12** again and you will see that the amount of memory allocated this time has changed to whatever you altered **Next** to.

If you had watched the **Free pool** slider previously when pressing **Ctrl-F12** you would have seen that each time you opened a Task Window the amount of free memory decreased by the amount of memory specified by **Next slot**.

At the bottom of the Task Manager window is a section labelled **Dynamic areas**. This is mainly for information only. A dynamic area is a part of the computer's memory used by a program to store data. These are created, extended and removed by programs as they are required. There is not normally anything that a user can or would need to do about these.

Killing tasks

If you click **MENU** over one of the task names in the Task Manager window the menu shown will open with the name of the task in the forth position from the top.

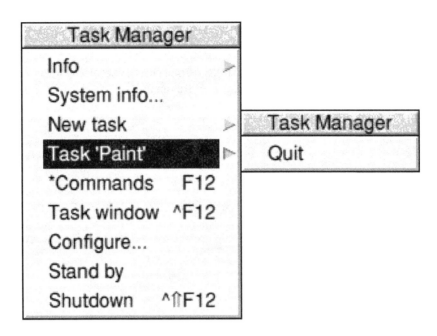

This menu has a sub-menu with just one item, **Quit** .

Almost all normal programs have a Quit item on their icon bar menu, but not all programs install on the icon bar. This is the way of killing those that don't. Just click on Quit and the task should die.

10. The Pinboard

The RISC OS desktop's background has two important features. Firstly it can have its appearance altered either by having a coloured backdrop, which can be graduated, a single large picture as the background to your desktop or by using a repeating pattern of a small graphics file or 'tile'. Altering the configuration of the Pinboard is covered in the Configuration Section of the RISC OS Six documentation.

The second function of the desktop backdrop is that it can act as a *pinboard*. If you drag a file, directory or application icon from a filer window onto the backdrop it will 'stick' there. The file on the disc hasn't been changed in any way, the icon on the backdrop is just a shortcut to the actual object on the disc. If you double click on it that will have the same effect as double-clicking on the 'real' icon on the disc; if it's a folder icon then a directory viewer will open, if it's an application then the application will be run.

You can put as many icons on the backdrop as you like, and can drag them around and arrange them as you choose.

Click the **MENU** button while the mouse pointer is anywhere over the backdrop and the pinboard menu will appear. If you select one or more icons then the **Selection** sub-menu can be accessed and from this you can 'tidy' the icons according to the configured **Choices** or **Remove** them completely.

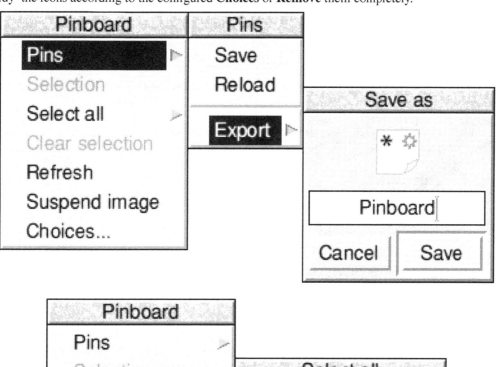

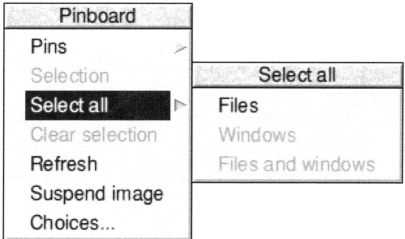

The main use of the pinboard is to hold application and folder icons that you use frequently. If they are placed on the pinboard they are always readily available even if they are deeply buried in a sub-sub-sub-directory on your hard drive.

When you have everything set up as you want it you can save your pinboard by clicking on **Save** in the **Pins** submenu. This will save the pinboard arrangement inside !Boot so that the next time you start up the computer the icons will be placed on your pinboard exactly as required.

If your Pinboard has become cluttered or you have changed it by mistake, you can click on **Reload** in the **Pins** submenu to restore it to the state it was last saved as.

For advanced use, you might want to have multiple pinboard files and be able to switch between them. The **Export** option on the **Pins** submenu allows you to save the current Pinboard file to a location of your choice. You could even pin these extra Pinboard files to each Pinboard layout and re-save them, so that you have an easy way to switch from one to another.

Tidy

As you drop various icons onto the pinboard, you may find that things get a little untidy. To resolve this little problem, you can use the **Tidy** option from the **Selection** submenu. This menu is only active once a selection has been made.

When you select **Tidy**, the selected objects will be neatly arranged according to your configured choices (see Configure section of the guide for details). You can temporarily override the configured options as you click **Tidy**, by holding down **Shift** and / or **Ctrl** on the keyboard.

Shift+Tidy will cause the selected objects to be tidied to the nearest corner of the screen to the mouse pointer.

Ctrl+Tidy will invert the configured stacking order, so if Vertical stacking was configured, then Horizontal stacking would be used instead.

Unavailable Pinned Objects

Pinboard now handles unavailable objects by representing them with the 'broken pinned object' icon shown above. Objects may be unavailable due to having been deleted, renamed, or being on removable media which is not currently available. Objects on Network shares might also fall into this category if the network resource is unavailable.

Versions of RISC OS prior to 6.10 simply removed any pins whose path was invalid when RISC OS was first booted, or left icons for files on the Pinboard if the file was removed during a session. The benefit of using the 'broken pinned object' icon is that you can place files from removable discs or from network shares into your Boot sequence. The files will initially be represented with the broken pin icon; as soon as you make the device available (eg. by logging into a network or by inserting the appropriate removeable device), you can click on the icon and use it normally.

If you have removed a removeable device or made changes to the locations of files which will affect your pins, you can click on **Refresh** on the main menu to check all the paths, and update the display. This will make it more obvious which files are available and which are not.

Suspend Image

Advanced users sometimes use their RISC OS computer remotely across a network, using programs such as *VNC viewers*. Whilst accessing a RISC OS machine in this way has many advantages, one of the major problems is that it is much slower to see updates to the screen. This delay is much worse if the computer has a large pinboard image. RISC OS 6.10 introduced the **Suspend Image** option on the Pinboard for this purpose. When selected, it temporarily removes the backdrop image to speed up the drawing of the screen. It does not change your permanent settings and the backdrop will be restored if the option is unselected, or if the computer is reset.

11. The Display Manager

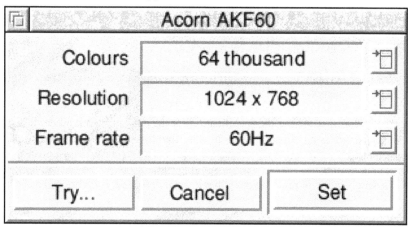 The Display Manager is used to select screen resolution, number of colours and other factors that affect how the desktop is displayed.

The **Display Manager** icon is immediately to the left of the **Task Manager** icon. If you click **SELECT** on this, a window similar to that shown will appear.

Acorn AKF60	
Colours	64 thousand
Resolution	1024 x 768
Frame rate	60Hz
Try...	Cancel	Set

The buttons to the right of the three: **Colours, Resolution** and **Frame rate** icons are known as *menu buttons*. If you click on any of them they will open a menu with a list of options from which you can choose to set that particular parameter.

If you click on the menu button beside **Colours** the menu shown will appear. Select any option from this menu and it will appear in the **Colours** icon.

Colours
- Black/white
- 4 greys
- 16 greys
- 16 colours
- 64 colours
- 256 greys
- 256 colours
- 32 thousand
- ✓ 64 thousand
- 16 million

Exactly what appears on these menus depends upon the monitor and driver your computer has been set up to use.

Any changes you make will not be enacted until you click on the **Set** button. To close the window without making any changes click the **Cancel** button.

If you want to see what the new screen mode you have chosen would look like, or even to check if it works on your monitor, you can first click on the **Try** button and RISC OS will switch to this mode for 10 seconds. If you get no screen display just wait (or press the Escape key) and your old screen mode will re-appear. Alternatively you can click **Set** to retain the mode.

If you click on the Display Manager icon with **MENU** then a menu will appear. This has a number of options:

Info will tell you which version of the display manager you are using.

Device will let you switch between display devices for which you have a driver. For example you could switch between the VIDC and a ViewFinder card.

Mode leads to a small window showing the specification for the current screen mode. It is possible to enter a *mode definition string* or an old style *mode number* into this window and click on the **OK** button to change to that screen mode.

A mode definition string is a line of text that describes a screen mode. It is composed as follows:

X1280 Y1024 C256 F75

This would give you an **X** resolution (width) of 1280 pixels, a **Y** resolution (height) of 1024 pixels, a Colour depth of 256 colours and a **F**rame rate of 75 Hz.

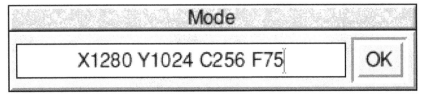

RISC OS Six adds further possible descriptors to the mode string. These are all prefixed by the letter **A**, for alias. For example say you have the monitor configured to a particular mode and want to alter just the colour depth. It's no longer necessary to use an entire mode string. Instead you can use the **A@** string. For example to keep all other elements the same but to alter the current colour depth you could use:

    A@ C16M

This will keep the X and Y resolutions and the frame rate, but set the current mode to have 16 million colours. You can use this process to alter any aspect of the mode, for example to keep all the details the same but to alter the frame rate:

    A@ F50

In addition you can also use the following new descriptors:

        N - Native mode of the monitor   C - User configured mode   @
    - Current mode

So as a further example, you could use **AN** to set the monitor to its native mode. Or **AN F75** to set the monitor to its default mode at 75 Hz.

Choices
Clicking on this will open the RISC OS Display Configuration window. If the monitor type is incorrectly

set it is possible that changing screen mode could result in some of the parameters being outside the range that your monitor can cope with and you are presented with a blank or 'scrambled' screen. If this happens then you will have to reset the computer to restore the default settings. If you use the **Try** button this is much less likely to be a problem.

12. The Apps icon

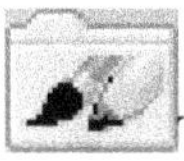

This icon is found on the icon bar to the right of all the disc drive icons. As the name implies it is intended to be used as an always available shortcut to applications. If you click on this icon it will open what appears to be a normal filer window, although it is a little bit different because it is for the read-only Resources filing system.

This Filer viewer behaves in the same way as other viewers in terms of its display type, sort order and keyboard short cuts, but does not give access to all the internal files within applications and does not let you copy files or applications to it.

The applications that will appear in the folder can be divided into two categories.

1. Applications that are part of RISC OS itself and are included in the RISC OS ROM, not on your hard disc.

2. Applications that you have installed on your hard disc but which can be made to appear here for easy access.

If you click on the Apps icon of a new RISC OS Six computer before any programs have been installed you should see something like the illustration below. You may have some different applications present, but you should always find the following:

- !Alarm

- !Chars

- !Configure

- !Draw

- !Edit

- !Help

- !Paint

- !SciCalc

- !Squash

If you search your hard drive you won't be able to find some of these programs because they are part of the RISC OS ROMs and the Apps icon is the only way that a user can access these programs to run them.

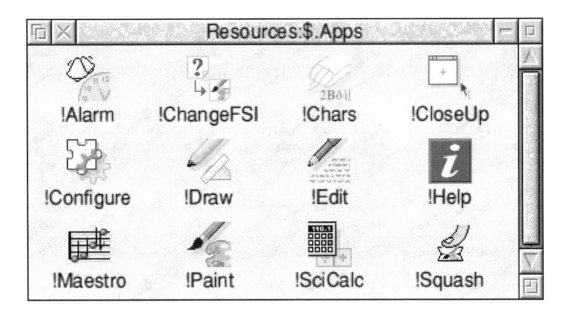

Because this is not a normal directory viewer you can't drag objects into it, so there has to be another way for you to get your own programs to appear here. In fact there are two ways.

The simplest way, and this also works with most earlier versions of RISC OS, is to place them in the **Apps** folder on your hard drive. You should find that in the root directory of your hard drive is a folder named **Apps** . If it isn't there you can just create it as described elsewhere. When the computer starts up this directory is scanned and any applications found there will also appear in Apps on the icon bar.

The second method is to use the Add to Apps facility of the RISC OS configuration system.

13. Printing

Printing can be one of the most frustrating parts of using a computer. One problem faced by the people who produce software is that there is a wide range of printers working with a wide range of computers; and they don't all work the same way.

The RISC OS Printer Manager application, !Printers, has been designed to present a unified interface and consistent interface to applications that need to print their output.

Hundreds of articles have been written about printing with RISC OS, and almost as many about the pro's and con's of the various types of printer - inkjet, mono laser, colour laser, solid ink, etc. and this is not the place to go into the subject in depth. This chapter will just describe very briefly how to set up and use a printer under RISC OS and some of the problems you might encounter.

Choosing a printer

This normally means choosing between an inkjet or laser printer.

Inkjets are usually cheaper to buy, especially if you need colour, but more expensive to run. There is another problem in that almost all inkjet printers require special rather than generic printer drivers. Many modern inkjets, especially low cost ones, can only be used with Windows or a Mac and not with RISC OS, so be sure to check before you buy that a RISC OS printer driver is available.

The warning about low cost printers only working on Windows or Macs also applies to laser printers, but things are slightly better as many laser printers will work using PCL5 or 6 or PostScript. The first is a proprietary Hewlett Packard printer language, systems and printers that support this (see the printer specification) will normally work with one of the HP Laserjet printer drivers supplied with RISC OS. Printers that support PostScript, both colour and mono, will usually work with the RISC OS PostScript printer driver.

In both these cases you may not be able to employ the full resolution or all the features of the printer but you should be able to use the printer at a basic level.

Unless you really know what you are doing you are strongly advised to seek expert advise from someone who understands printing with RISC OS before purchasing a printer.

Installing !Printers

The !Printers application and the printer drivers supplied with it should be found in the **Printing** directory of the root directory of your hard disc. The contents of this directory should look like this;

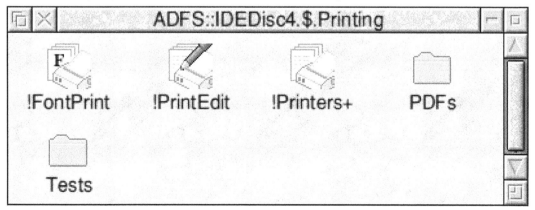

!FontPrint is a utility for setting up fonts used by PostScript printers. It has its own !Help file and if you are using a PostScript printer it is worthwhile installing !FontPrint otherwise you will not need it.

!Printers or **!Printers+** is the actual printing application. Double click on it and it will install on the icon bar. At this stage it can't be used, no printer driver has been installed. The icon will look like the one below with the word 'Printers' below it.

Printer drivers are in the **PDFs** sub-directory of the **Printing** directory. Here you will find a lot more directories, one for each make of printer, plus PostScript printer drivers. To illustrate how a printer driver is installed, open the **Canon** directory. Part of what you will see is shown below. Each of these files is a *Printer Definition File* or PDF for a model of printer. Drag the file **BJC-800** to the Printer icon on the icon bar. It will be recognised as a PDF and loaded by the Printer program and the icon will change to show that it is active. You will also see that the name of the printer driver will appear under the icon.

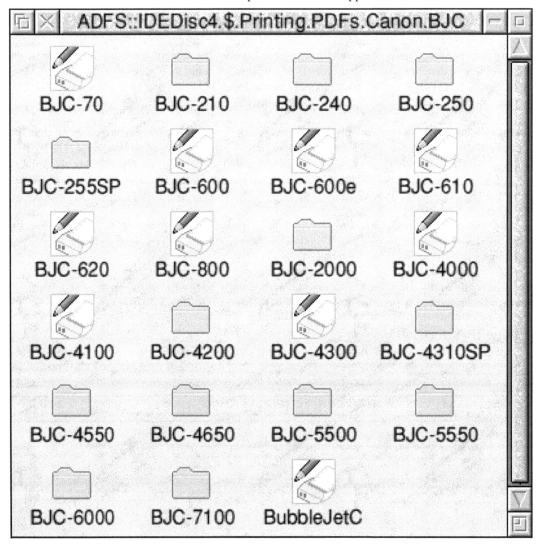

Click **MENU** on the icon and the menu shown below will appear.

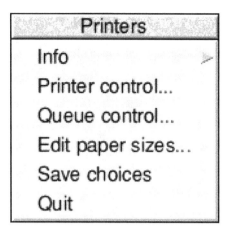

Click on **Printer control** and the window shown below will open. This gives brief information about the printer driver and tells you that it is the *Active driver*. (More about this later).

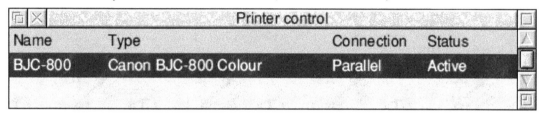

Close this window and click on **Queue control.** This will open the window below. Not a lot is going on here at the moment but if you click **MENU** over this window the menu that appears will give you some idea of its purpose.

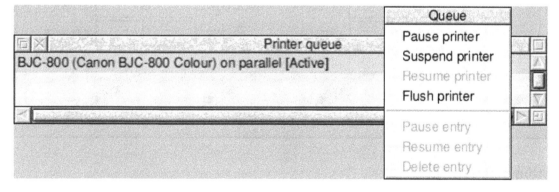

When you begin printing each 'print job' is placed in a queue, and that queue is shown in this window. The reason for the queuing system is because printing can take some time, and if you wanted to print, say, three separate pages of text, instead of waiting for each page to finish before telling the printer to print the next you could tell it to print all three, one after the other. They would then be placed in the queue and would be printed one at a time.

The purpose of the queue window is not only to tell you what is in the queue but to give you control over it. If you change your mind about one of the items you can delete it before it's printed, or you can 'flush' the printer, that is, stop whatever it's doing and delete everything in the queue.

If you select **Edit paper sizes** from the menu the window shown below will appear. This lets you set the paper size and margins. If you are using the right driver for your printer then these settings should be correct, unless you want to use a different paper size such as Legal. If you are using a slightly different driver, that is, one known to work with your printer but not the exact driver, then you should check the settings for the margins with your printer specification. This is particularly likely to be the case with laser printers, especially PostScript since these are generic drivers, not specific to your printer. Also modern inkjets can often print closer to the edges of the paper than older models so you may be able to reduce the margins.

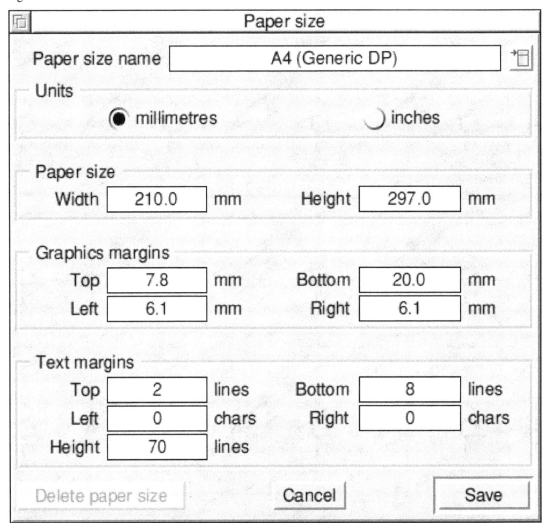

Setting your choices

When you have set everything as you want it click on **Save choices** on the printer menu. This will save your settings inside !Boot and the next time you run !Printers it will start up with the correct driver, paper size, etc. ready to use.

Multiple printers

It is now common for people to have both a mono laser printer for correspondence and a colour inkjet for printing pictures and use a two way switch in the printer lead to switch between them.

It would be inconvenient to have to install a complete new printer driver every time you changed printer. To install more than one printer driver, proceed as described above and install the driver for the first printer. Now open the Printer control window and drag the PDF for the second printer to the window. The information for the second printer will appear there and you will see that a second printer icon has appeared on the icon bar beside the first.

This icon will be pale grey. If you click on it its colour will change, the original icon will become pale grey and you will see that the highlighted printer in the Printer control window changes.

You can now set up the second printer as previously described.

When you print anything the active printer driver is the one that will be used, that is, the one with the coloured icon on the icon bar, and you switch between them by just clicking on the icon for the printer you require.

When you have everything set click on **Save choices** just as before. You should note that whatever printer was active when you did this will be the one selected when you next run !Printers.

Don't forget to change both the printer switch and the printer driver when you change printers or you will get some very strange results.

This is also a good way to alternate between A4 and A3 paper sizes if you are using an A3 printer. Set the paper size on one printer to A4 and the other to A3. You will see that this has already been done for you with some of the Canon printer drivers.

Direct Printing

Most of the time you will be printing directly from an application, but there may be times when you want to print a file without loading it into the program. The !Printer program can do this for some common file types such as a Draw or Text file.

Just drag the file icon to the printer icon on the icon bar and it will be printed.

14. Quit an application

Normally you would quit an application using the **Quit** from its iconbar menu. However sometimes it is possible for an application to go wrong and refuse to quit. If you do have a problem with an application, you could try holding the **Alt** key on the keyboard and pressing the **Break** key. The RISC OS task manager will bring up a window asking if you want to quit the current task. If the task shown is the wrong one you can cycle through all the running tasks by repeatedly clicking on the **Next Task** button. Once you have found the task you want to quit, click on the **Stop** button.

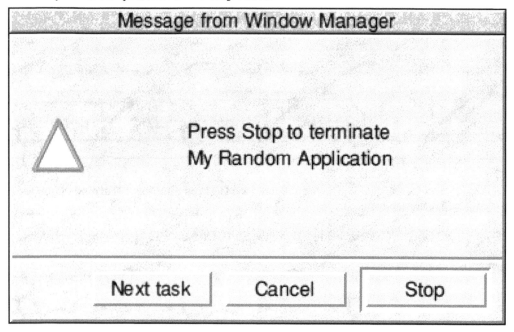

Shutting down

At some point you will need to shutdown or reset the computer.

If you do need to switch off the computer then you should shutdown RISC OS correctly. Just turning the power off at the wall is not recommended as the computer could be busy doing things and you could corrupt your harddisc as well as lose any work that you are currently doing.

RISC OS Six includes a shutdown menu option. Click with the **MENU** button on the Task Manager icon, then click on '**Shutdown**' on the menu which will appear. The following window will then be shown:

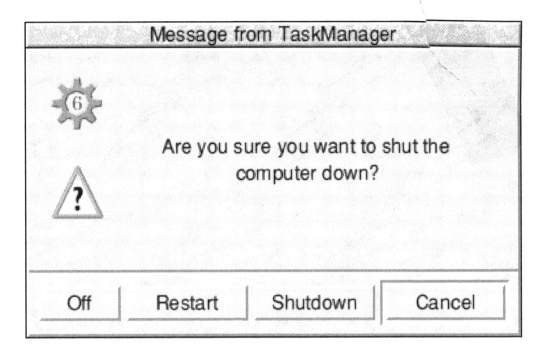

If you don't see this window then you have configured the **Desktop Shutdown Warning** option to be off in configuration settings of RISC OS.

You can also shutdown RISC OS by holding down the **Shift**, **Ctrl** and **F12** keys on the keyboard.

You now have a number of choices.

Cancel - click on this if you don't want to shut down.

Shutdown - click on this to close down RISC OS, you can then turn your computer off.

Restart - this will shutdown then restart RISC OS.

Off - if your computer supports power management then this will shutdown RISC OS and turn the computer off.

Stand by

If your computer supports it then RISC OS Six can put the machine into **Stand by** mode. The computer will appear to shut down as normally, except that some components will go into power saving mode. Files that you still have open will be preserved in memory. You can then restart the machine and it will start up much quicker and the RISC OS desktop will appear exactly as it was when you clicked on **Stand by**. We recommend that this option is used with caution, for example if you have a power cut whilst the machine is in this mode then your open work could be lost.

www.ingramcontent.com/pod-product-compliance
Lightning Source LLC
Chambersburg PA
CBHW080601060326
40689CB00021B/4902